PRAISE
Agile Conversations

"I think of this highly practical and immediately applicable book as the lost instruction manual to the most powerful and effective Agile tool we don't even realize we have: Conversations. If you want to be successful with Agile, RTFM: Read This Fabulous Manual."

—**Alberto Savoia**, Google's first Director of Engineering
and Author of *The Right It*

"*Agile Conversations* provides much needed guidance on how to have the key discussions that form the foundation for strong and resilient working relationships, as well as a toolbox full of techniques for troubleshooting when conversations go awry. Full of practical, real-world examples, this book is a must read for anyone who has ever been frustrated or puzzled by interactions at work."

—**Elisabeth Hendrickson**, Technology Executive
and Author of *Explore It!*

"Many books have been written about improving process and product in companies. I'm so glad this book finally addresses the people aspect: Learn to ask the hard questions, leave your bias at the door, and improve your own communication with this practical guide. If it's hard, do it more often!"

—**Patrick Debois**, Founder of DevOpsDays and
Co-Author of *The DevOps Handbook*

"This book provides an engineer's approach to monitoring, troubleshooting, and debugging conversations.... Heuristics such as the Question Fraction are amazing—at the same time simple and memorable and incredibly insightful. Read this book to turn your communication skills into superpowers."

—**Gojko Adžić**, Author, and Partner at Neuri Consulting

"Vital reading for anyone in a leadership role or interested in improving their work culture in general."

—**Andy Skipper**, Chief Coach at CTO Craft

"If you're looking for a practical framework and techniques that will help fix broken team communication and dysfunctional culture, then you should read *Agile Conversations*. Going beyond simple diagnosis, this handbook walks you through the Five Conversations you need to embrace in order to transform a broken culture into one that's healthy and high-performing."

—**Paul Joyce**, Founder and CEO, Geckoboard

"Squirrel and Jeffrey's keen writing and battle-tested techniques make this book a must-read for modern engineering leaders looking to thrive amid the explosion of complexity that we all face."

—**Chris Clearfield**, Co-Author of *Meltdown: What Plane Crashes, Oil Spills, and Dumb Business Decisions Can Teach Us About How to Succeed at Work and at Home*

"This is a very wise and yet readable book. The authors have hit the nail on the head by focusing on better conversations as the way to translate theory into organizational improvement."

—**Rich Koppel**, Co-Founder and CEO of TIM Group

"It's one of the industry's dirty little secrets that most of our 'technology' problems are actually people problems. In *Agile Conversations*, Jeffrey and Squirrel assert that solving these problems is made possible by having better conversations, presenting their advice in a manner which fellow technologists will find reassuringly structured and categorized."

—**Jon Topper**, Founder & CEO, The Scale Factory

"It takes conviction and skill to change company culture. *Agile Conversations* provides the road map to summon your courage and avoid the hazards on your path to success! A masterpiece for any CEO wanting to build a collaborative, cooperative organization!"

—**Brent Delehey**, Turnaround Specialist, CEO

"This book is an extremely helpful and practical guide on how to read between your own lines, and make it safe for others to reveal the fears between theirs."

—**Rebecca Williams**, Software Engineer at QA Chef

Agile Conversations

Transform Your Conversations, Transform Your Culture

DOUGLAS SQUIRREL
and **JEFFREY FREDRICK**

IT Revolution
Independent Publisher Since 2013
Portland, Oregon

25 NW 23rd Pl, Suite 6314
Portland, OR 97210

First Edition
Printed in the United States of America
25 24 23 22 21 20   1 2 3 4 5 6 7 8 9 10

Cover and book design by Devon Smith

Library of Congress Catalog-in-Publication Data

Names: Squirrel, Douglas, author. | Fredrick, Jeffrey, author.
Title: Agile conversations : transform your conservations, transform your culture / by Douglas Squirrel and Jeffrey Fredrick.
Description: First edition. | Portland, Oregon : IT Revolution, [2020] | Includes bibliographical references.
Identifiers: LCCN 2019045822 (print) | LCCN 2019045823 (ebook) | ISBN 9781942788973 (paperback) | ISBN 9781942788669 (epub) | ISBN 9781942788676 (kindle edition) | ISBN 9781942788683 (pdf)
Subjects: LCSH: Communication in management. | Teams in the workplace. | Information technology—management.
Classification: LCC HD30.3 .S698 2020 (print) | LCC HD30.3 (ebook) | DDC 658.4/5—dc23
LC record available at https://lccn.loc.gov/2019045822
LC ebook record available at https://lccn.loc.gov/2019045823

ISBN: 978-1942788973
eBook ISBN: 978-1942788669
Kindle ISBN: 978-1942788676
Web PDF ISBN: 978-1942788683

For information about special discounts for bulk purchases or for information on booking authors for an event, please visit our website at ITRevolution.com.

Names have been changed in example conversations and stories for privacy.

AGILE CONVERSATIONS

For Leanne and Lisa.

Contents

Figures and Tables

Introduction

A Word from the Authors

As a leader at your company, you've given the transformation your full support, and the organization has bought in. You've had the consultants in, they've trained the teams, and the process is in place. All that's missing are the promised results. Why aren't things better?

As a contributor—an engineer, product owner, Scrum Master, system admin, tech lead, tester, or any other "doer"—you've had the training, written the tickets, and gone to the meetings. You've bought in and are ready to see improvements. All that's missing are the promised results. Why aren't things better?

After years of study and many missteps, we have come to understand that the key to success is not only *adopting practices* but *having the difficult conversations* that foster the right environment for those practices to work. You, your managers, and your teams are missing the right relationships, built only by having the right conversations. The good news is that you can begin a conversational transformation that builds the foundation for any other improvements you want to make, changing your conversations, improving your relationships, and finally getting results.

We've seen it happen. Between us, we've consulted with over one hundred organizations across a range of subjects and at all levels. It has been our surprising experience that no matter whether we are talking with a CEO or the most junior developer, a managing director at a multinational bank or an operations engineer at an online retailer, a product owner or a project manager, a designer or a developer, in every case we hear, "Why won't *he* do it better? Why won't *she* change? I can't make them. I'm powerless."

Employees' frustration and despair at their inability to change things exist at all levels and in almost all organizations we've worked with—and we feel empathy, because we get stuck in this pattern ourselves.

So it has been our great joy to offer an alternative: the tremendous power of conversations based on transparency and curiosity.

We have regularly and reliably seen individuals, teams, and whole organizations get unstuck and start seeing improvements faster than they thought possible when they unlocked their conversational superpowers: a children's book publisher that got artists and marketers talking and harnessed creative inspiration for successful sales; an AI startup that involved everyone in setting strategy, seeing big improvements in user satisfaction; a financial-services firm that stabilized its systems through tough discussions of its failings.

Great results follow when you learn that a conversation is about more than just talking; it is a skilled activity. There is more to a conversation than what you can see and hear. In addition to what is said out loud, there is what has been left unsaid—the thoughts and feelings behind our spoken and unspoken words.

As we become more skillful at conversations, we become more aware of *what* we think and feel, and *why* we think and feel the way we do. Therefore, we become better at sharing that information with others. We also become more aware that we don't have telepathy—that we don't actually know what information our conversational partners have—so we get better at asking questions and listening to the answers. These skills are so fundamental, and so neglected, that when we get better at them, our conversations become radically more productive and our culture becomes much more collaborative.

There is no shortage of books that tell you how to *diagnose* cultural problems, offering detailed case studies and stories, diagnostic tests, lots of practices to follow, exhortations to collaborate, and tools to use. But few say anything meaningful about how you actually cure those problems—how to make changes and what to do when you're stuck.

For example, Patrick Lencioni's *The Five Dysfunctions of a Team: A Leadership Fable* details the fall and rise of the fictional company DecisionTech. Through this corporate fable, Lencioni develops a theory of dysfunctional hierarchy: Inattention to Results arises from Avoidance of Accountability, which, in turn, is rooted in a Lack of Commitment, and so on through Fear of Conflict and Absence of Trust.[1] Lencioni's model of dysfunction is helpful, and it inspired four of our Five Conversations (which you'll learn about later in this book). But crucially, Lencioni offers little practical advice for removing dysfunction once you find it.

To build trust, he says, you can do one of five things: share your personal history, discuss your team members' most important strengths and weaknesses, provide feedback, run personality type analyses, or go on a ropes course.[2] While these are likely to make your team more friendly or intimate, Lencioni offers no evidence or argument that they will actually create trust, nor does he provide any alternatives for building trust if they fail.

Lencioni is not alone in hanging the reader out to dry in this way. Business fables, digital transformation guides, Agile manuals—all of them tell you what's wrong with your culture but not how to fix it. As a result, we have seen company after company implement all the right practices but fail to see results because they haven't fixed their cultural glue, the very thing necessary to make those other practices work.

This book and the use of our conversational methods will teach you and your team to not only diagnose your cultural problems but actually cure them. We have seen over and over that holding difficult conversations with an attitude of transparency and curiosity *does* help teams build lasting trust, reduce fear, and make other key improvements; and that it's easy to explain how and why this method works, which is what we will do in this book.

If you have the appetite, you can develop the skills that allow you to embrace the *painful, candid communication* that creates an environment in which teams flourish. At no point will developing these skills be easy. In the words of our friend Mark Coleman, it will demand "difficult, emotional work"[3] from you at every stage. You will have to confront your own dread of painful topics—and more than once, instead of taking on yet another challenging discussion, you will wish you could just bring in a consultant, or polish your burndown chart, or add some monitoring. But we can assure you that there is nothing as rewarding as working in an organization whose members have mastered all of the Five Conversations, and for whom the never-ending quest for excellence is a habit and a joy.

We look forward to you joining us in learning, developing, and implementing the conversational skills that get you there.

Keep talking,
Jeffrey and Squirrel

How This Book Is Organized

We've divided the book into two parts: Part I describes the ideas and theories that underpin the conversational tools that we will introduce in Part II.

Chapter 1 is a bit of software history. If you want to get directly to techniques, you can skip this chapter; but if you are curious about the origins of Agile, Lean, and DevOps, this chapter is for you. We will examine the dramatic changes that have transformed the software industry over the last twenty-five years, recapping what we lived through, including both the progress and stumbles along the way.

In the 1990s the mass manufacturing paradigm provided the intellectual model for the "software factory." Just as factory workers were expected to be interchangeable units, bound to the assembly line, so, too, were software professionals expected to be interchangeable units, following the dictates of the document-driven approach to software development. When that model proved disastrously flawed in practice, it created space for the rise of a host of people-centric methodologies and the waves of transformations that have swept across software organizations, such as Agile, Lean, and DevOps.

Ironically, as commonly implemented as these transformations are, they often miss the people-centric core, and a bureaucratic focus on processes and practices leaves organizations stuck with cultureless rituals. To advance, organizations will need to tap into the unique human power of conversations, overcoming their cognitive biases by learning to have difficult but productive conversations.

Chapter 2 provides the core techniques of our method: the Four Rs provide steps to help us learn from our conversations, and the Two-Column Conversational Analysis gives us both a format we use throughout the book for recording conversations and a method for learning from them. We recommend reading at least the two sections on these techniques and the section "Analyzing a Conversation" before proceeding.

We start the chapter by showing that you already know where you need to go. Following illustrious social scientist Chris Argyris, we'll show you that your "espoused theory" already says that the best decisions require collaboration, transparency, and curiosity from all involved. Unfortunately, your "theory in use," how you actually behave in conversations, is something quite different. We will show you a method called "the Four Rs," a set of techniques that allow anyone and any team to improve their skills in approaching difficult topics in their conversations, which will help you learn from your conversations and prepare for what comes next.

In Part II, Chapters 3 through 7, we've distilled our experience, learnings, and mistakes into an "instruction manual" for the Five Conversations: crucial discussions of the five key characteristics that *all* high-performing teams share not just software teams but all human teams.

The Five Conversations are:

1. **The Trust Conversation:** We hold a belief that those we work with, inside and outside the team, share our goals and values.
2. **The Fear Conversation:** We openly discuss problems in our team and its environment and courageously attack those obstacles.
3. **The Why Conversation:** We share a common, explicit purpose that inspires us.
4. **The Commitment Conversation:** We regularly and reliably announce what we will do and when.
5. **The Accountability Conversation:** We radiate our intent to all interested parties and explain publicly how our results stack up against commitments.*

These five conversations address attributes that give teams everything they need to exploit modern, people-centric practices to the hilt. With them it is possible to achieve elite-level delivery speeds, fearlessly adjusting on the fly and committing to show real customers working software that solves their problems. And these are exactly the characteristics missing from the teams we see too often today, where standups are places to hide progress rather than share it, where estimation is a forlorn exercise in futility, where the team's purpose is lost in a sea of tickets, and where frustration is the shared emotion from one end of the organization to the other.

Starting with the Trust Conversation, and continuing with conversations addressing Fear, Why, Commitment, and Accountability, we will show you in

---

* Four of the Five Conversations were inspired by the Five Dysfunctions identified by Patrick Lencioni.[4] The fifth, the Why Conversation, was inspired by Simon Sinek's *Start with Why: How Great Leaders Inspire Everyone to Take Action*.[5] To each we have added our own experiences and approaches, and we are grateful to both authors for their inspiration.

detail and step by step how to improve each of these five key attributes in your team. You'll be able to use these methods whether you are a junior developer or a senior executive, and we'll explain how these improvements will translate directly into improved results from your Agile, Lean, and DevOps practices. We'll illustrate how these methods work in real life, with practical examples of conversations on each topic.

Chapters 3 through 7 are each divided into similar sections:

- A *motivational* section explaining why the chapter's featured conversation is important.
- A *story* section introducing a protagonist experiencing a problematic conversation of this type.
- One or more *preparation* sections that teach you methods introduced in the chapter's conversation.
- An *explanatory* section ("The Conversation") that describes one way to hold the chapter's conversation.
- A section that *continues the story*, where our protagonist learns from the problematic conversation and produces a better result.
- Several *example conversations* that illustrate variations on the chapter's conversation.
- A *case study*, which tells a longer story about how the chapter's conversation helped an organization improve.

But reading to the end of the book is only the beginning. Having learned how to approach each of the key conversations, it will be up to you to practice what you've learned. If you do, we are confident you'll find the effort rewarded many times over. When you transform your conversations, you transform your culture.

The Many Ways to Read This Book

Perl developers have a catchy acronym: "TIMTOWTDI," or "there is more than one way to do it." That's our philosophy, as you'll see throughout this book; so long as you address the Five Conversations in one way or another, we aren't prescriptive about which practices you use. We think answers to questions like how long your iterations should be, whether you need standups, or what color of planning poker cards to use are less important than how you get to those answers. Similarly, we've tried to write this book so you can use it in multiple ways, depending on your learning style, needs, or mood.

So here are some suggestions for ways to read the book, but TIMTOWTDI, so we don't mind if you come up with your own!

> ***Linear.*** If you like to understand every idea the first time you encounter it, this is the method for you: start at page one and keep reading until you run out of pages. We've tried to define and illustrate each new idea or technique before using it, avoiding forward references wherever possible. So if you master Test-Driven Development for People in the Trust Conversation, you won't have trouble when it crops up two chapters later in the Why Conversation. And within each chapter, you'll find the kind of logical progression you like: first the reason for having that chapter's conversation, then techniques to use it, followed by the conversation itself, and finally practical examples. Reinforce your learning by using the Four Rs to work through the sample conversations at the end of each chapter and your own examples. Involve one or more friends in your step-by-step learning if you can.

> ***Technical.*** "Don't confuse me with stories; get to the methods I can use." If this is you, then start in the preparation section of each chapter, where we explain techniques you can begin practicing immediately to improve your conversations and, therefore, your team's performance. Keep reading through the explanation of the main conversation, which brings the techniques together into a whole, until you get to the example conversations, which illustrate the conversation in action, and from which you can lift phrases and approaches. Having chosen this path, we recommend you proceed at the rate of no more than one method per week, and spend each week deliberately practicing the methods in your everyday conversations. At the end of each day, make a count of how often you were able to apply each method, and choose one conversation to analyze using the Four Rs. Outwardly slow and steady, this reflective practice will quickly build skills if you stick with it.

> ***Social.*** As we describe in the Conclusion, other people who are also interested in learning these skills can be a tremendous aid in learning the material. The cognitive biases that make these conversations

difficult also make it more difficult to spot our own mistakes. Other people will have no such difficulty! If you are fortunate enough to have such a learning group, we would recommend that, as a group, you follow a similar path as the Technical approach on the previous page. Cover no more than one chapter per week, keep and share your count of how often you could apply the methods of that chapter, and then discuss and analyze one of your conversations in a group session. Role playing and reversing roles with others will help you gain confidence in your performance; the practice of giving feedback to others will help you spot opportunities for improvement in your own conversations.

Whatever approach you take to reading the book, it is worth emphasizing that understanding is simply not enough; you build the skills by practicing. There is no other way.

Part I

Chapter 1

Escaping the Software Factory

According to Michael Gale, author of *The Digital Helix: Transforming Your Organization's DNA to Thrive in the Digital Age*, 84% of digital transformations fail.[1] Trying to understand why the other 16% succeed, he found that success required a "fundamental shift in how people had to think about how they interact, how they collaborate and work, and if you don't spend time changing people's behaviors, you don't spend time changing culture and how people make decisions, all of this falls flat."[2]

Our way to make this fundamental shift is to turn to the most human of abilities: the conversation. Humans have a uniquely powerful and flexible language. To get the most out of it, we need to learn the skill of conversation and how to overcome our innate biases, which work against collaboration and connection. When we change our conversations, we change our culture.

To understand the change we need, it helps to understand the culture we are coming from. As we describe in this chapter, we are still in the process of emerging from the mass-manufacturing paradigm of the software factory. This document-only model represents an attempt at communication without conversation. The failure of the software factory model has created space for the rise of new, people-centric models like Agile, Lean, and DevOps. But well-meaning attempts to adopt these new models fail when the focus is on processes and methods, reinventing some of the same mistakes of the software factory on a smaller scale, creating "feature factories," as John Cutler calls them.[3]

Laboring in the Software Factory

We both began our careers in the 1990s in medium-size software companies,* wrangling C code on huge, desk-bound PCs alongside dozens or hundreds of our colleagues doing the same thing. We were small parts embedded in a much larger system. And no wonder, since the systems we were part of were an expression of the twentieth-century philosophy known as Taylorism.

A machinist and mechanical engineer by trade, Frederick Winslow Taylor led a professional crusade against waste and inefficiency, becoming one of the first management consultants in the process. At the heart of the waste, in Taylor's mind, was the wide variation in how work was performed from one worker to the next. It would be much better, he reasoned, for everyone to be taught the one right way, and then for workers to follow that way without deviation; any other approach must necessarily be less efficient. And who determined the one right way? Professional managers and consultants such as Taylor himself.

"Scientific management," the philosophy of which Taylor was the most vocal proponent, says that it is the job of managers to devise and understand the best way of working and then enforce unswerving standardization. With his influential 1911 book *The Principles of Scientific Management*, Taylor provided the intellectual underpinning for mass manufacturing based on the assembly line, with low-skilled workers doing the same simple tasks again and again under the watchful eye of management.[4]

Taylor's view of the world created a very distinctive and dehumanizing workplace culture. The factory was envisioned as one giant machine. Managers were the mechanical engineers, designing how all the pieces should work and checking that they were operating correctly. Workers were merely replaceable parts: they operated within specified tolerances, or they were defective and to be discarded. Communication was top-down and limited to commands and corrections. Conversations were not required. Collaboration

* Jeffrey at Borland, Squirrel at Tenfold. Both have long since been swallowed by bigger fish.

was not required. Thought was not required beyond doing the job you had been told to do.

Taylorism in the Cubicle

The software industry we joined in the nineties had transplanted Taylor from the factory into the cubicle. Consultants and salesmen promised managers ease and efficiency in the new tools, new processes, and new methodologies they were peddling. "Having trouble with software development? Bugs and delays got you down? Never fear! We have the best practices written down and ready to go." Management could buy the system off the shelf and tell developers to follow along. And as the work flowed through every defined checkpoint and process gate, you could be confident that you would be on time and on budget. Or so was the promise.

Lacking a mechanical assembly line, the software industry created one from paper. Managers adopted or invented logical models describing the single, right way to work and codified them in documents with step-by-step instructions and flowcharts. This documentation-driven development was designed to stamp out any possibility for error by specifying how each part of the final program would function and what each software worker would do to make it happen. There was the marketing requirements document, the product specification, the architecture documentation, the implementation specification, the test plans, and more—no human activity was left unaccounted for. Thick manuals prescribed in painstaking detail the attributes of every data structure, which language constructs could be used, and even the format of comments. Meticulous software designs arrived on designers' desks, with every database column specified, every validation defined, and each screen carefully illustrated down to the last pixel.

But there *was* a logic to this. Everyone knew it was more expensive to fix defects after the software was shipped to clients. In fact, the earlier we found the bugs, the cheaper they were to fix. It was less effort to fix the designers' flowchart than to fix the code, and less effort still to update the specification document than to change the flowchart. The inexorable logic dictated that we should spend the time up front to get everything right, and then mechanically implement to save ourselves time and money downstream. It was all very sensible, all very rational.

Unfortunately, it didn't work very well.

The Software Crisis

Just how poorly this system worked was documented by the Standish Group in their infamous 1994 *CHAOS Report* on the shocking level of failure in software projects. Unlike the failures of bridges or airplanes or nuclear plants, the authors noted that "in the computer industry . . . failures are covered up, ignored, and/or rationalized." So they set out to identify "the scope of project failures," "the major factors that cause software projects to fail," and "the key ingredients that can reduce project failures." The report concluded that 31% of software projects in the United States were cancelled, costing American software companies $81 billion. Only 16% of projects were completed on time and on budget.[5] The report laid bare the failures of Taylorist methods and the software crisis they had created.

With the crisis widely acknowledged, there was no shortage of people searching for answers. One school of thought was captured in the Capability Maturity Model (CMM) from the Software Engineering Institute at Carnegie Mellon University. Created to help the US Department of Defense assess software contractors, CMM doubled down on the importance of documentation and process. Adherents of this approach implemented greater supervision, more checks, and additional specifications in their quest for predictability. "A software development process which is under statistical control will . . . produce the desired results within the anticipated limits of cost, schedule and quality," they asserted.[6]

Others from across the software industry, including software practitioners on the ground and those working with them, found inspiration and ideas in other places. Being on the front line of projects, they had the scars showing that the idealized, mechanical approach, no matter how reasonable it sounded, didn't explain why software projects succeeded or failed. Rather than working from first principles, they observed what worked in practice. In trying to understand their experiences, they found the answer couldn't be captured in reams of documentation. It wasn't a tool you could buy, and it wasn't in the mechanical application of process. It was *people*!

Dr. Alistair Cockburn, a keen and eloquent observer of software practices in the wild, captured the insight in his paper "Characterizing People as Non-Linear, First-Order Components in Software Development." The title tells the story. In stark contrast with the CMM, Cockburn said he, "now consider[s] process factors to be second-order issues."[7] He found that it was largely people who make projects succeed or fail, and suggested we focus our improvement efforts on harnessing the unique attributes of people.[8] For example:

> 1. People are communicating beings, doing best face-to-face, in person, with real-time question[s] and answer[s].
> 2. People have trouble acting consistently over time.
> 3. People are highly variable, varying from day to day and place to place.
> 4. People generally want to be good citizens—are good at looking around, taking initiative, and doing "whatever is needed" to get the project to work.[9]

This view of people is antithetical to the Taylorist view of people as mechanical, interchangeable parts. Expecting them to act as such ignores human nature and is doomed to failure. The empirical finding was that the culture of how people relate to one another and how they communicate on projects was important. Practitioners could see that we should be designing approaches and projects around people, not processes. We needed to be having the right conversations, building the right culture, if we wanted to improve our chances of success.

Smash the Machines—Maybe?

The idea that people are the central concern of software methods sparked an extended transformation that has reshaped the building of software since the turn of the century. Lean manufacturing disrupted and transformed the previously dominant Taylorist mass-manufacturing paradigm, scoring tremendous gains in productivity and quality by changing the culture of the factory. Rather than viewing workers as replaceable parts, Lean manufacturing relies on "both an extremely skilled and a highly motivated workforce," one that anticipates problems and devises solutions.[10]

Agile software development, Lean software, and DevOps have similarly disrupted and transformed the software factory. Each of these approaches targeted different elements of the factory, but they all started with a break from the dehumanizing, mass-manufacturing approach. They changed the culture by breaking down divisions of labor and introducing collaboration in the place of rigid process.

As we're about to illustrate in the following sections, the early proponents in each movement implicitly espoused two fundamental values, *transparency* and *curiosity*, which led them to advocate methods that developed some or all of our five key attributes of successful software teams: high trust, low fear, understanding why, making commitments, and being accountable. And these values and attributes were all about human connections, information flow, eliminating barriers, and collaboration—everything the software factory wasn't.

The initial wins from each successive movement were amazing: early adopters reported dramatic improvements in time to market, reduced bug rates, and higher team morale. The Lean Startup advocates, for example, boasted about "doing the impossible [releasing to production] fifty times a day."[11] Unsurprisingly, many others, including both of us, climbed on the bandwagon and tried the new methods to see if we could get the same results.

The problem—and the reason for this book—is that during the explosion of Agile development, and then of Lean software and DevOps, later adopters missed the importance of human interaction. Leaders thought they could behave the same as they always had—could keep their factory mind-set—and that dictating change to others would be enough. As a result, they focused on the easily monitored, more superficial process changes: standups, work-in-progress limits, tool selection.

Without the human element and without the right conversations, these changes were singularly ineffective. As a result, across hundreds of organizations between us, we've repeatedly seen disillusioned executives and frustrated teams declaring that Agile development (or Lean software or DevOps) *just doesn't work.*

To summarize, they took a mechanistic view of joining the human-centric transformation, missed or denied the importance of relationships, and then wondered why nobody was cooperating and nothing was getting done.

This book, by contrast, is all about getting back to the basic human interactions you'll need to succeed. Let's start by reviewing the history of each movement, which will prepare us to look at the simple technique you need to master to get people back into your process: the conversation.

Agile: People-Driven Development

By the end of the 1990s, the rebellion against the software factory had produced a Cambrian explosion of alternative approaches to software. Bucking the dominant paradigm of "documentation driven, heavyweight software development processes,"[12] the members of the new movements advocated heretical practices like just-in-time design, frequent delivery of working software, and involvement of real customers in software production. Most extreme was a cultural change that called for a radical reduction in planning activities in favor of collaborative interactions between individuals doing the work. To those used to the dominant practices of the software factory, these leaders seemed like a crazed mob bent on creating mayhem. And yet there were stories of amazing results—elevated morale, rapid delivery, high quality—in the teams brave enough to try these new methods.

Then, seventeen of the most visible proponents of the "lightweight software" movement gathered at the ski resort in Snowbird, Utah, in February 2001. As documented by James Highsmith, they were a diverse group, including the founders and advocates of Extreme Programming (XP), SCRUM, DSDM, Adaptive Software Development (ASD), Crystal, Feature-Driven Development (FDD), Pragmatic Programming, and others.[13] The question was, could they find common ground?

As it turns out, they did, and the result was, as Martin Fowler said, a "call to arms," a "rallying cry":[14] the Agile Manifesto, which continues to be widely used nearly two decades later.

> **Manifesto for Agile Software Development**
>
> We are uncovering better ways of developing software by doing it and helping others do it. Through this work we have come to value:
>
> - **Individuals and interactions** over processes and tools
> - **Working software** over comprehensive documentation
> - **Customer collaboration** over contract negotiation
> - **Responding to change** over following a plan
>
> That is, while there is value in the items on the right, we value the items on the left more.[15]

The group followed the manifesto with an often-overlooked set of twelve accompanying principles. This set of principles remains a useful touchpoint for organizations who aim for agility.

We follow these principles:

Our highest priority is to satisfy the customer through early and continuous delivery of valuable software.

Welcome changing requirements, even late in development. Agile processes harness change for the customer's competitive advantage.

Deliver working software frequently, from a couple of weeks to a couple of months, with a preference to the shorter timescale.

Business people and developers must work together daily throughout the project.

Build projects around motivated individuals. Give them the environment and support they need, and trust them to get the job done.

The most efficient and effective method of conveying information to and within a development team is face-to-face conversation.

Working software is the primary measure of progress.

Agile processes promote sustainable development. The sponsors, developers, and users should be able to maintain a constant pace indefinitely.

Continuous attention to technical excellence and good design enhances agility.

Simplicity—the art of maximizing the amount of work not done—is essential.

The best architectures, requirements, and designs emerge from self-organizing teams.

At regular intervals, the team reflects on how to become more effective, then tunes and adjusts its behavior accordingly.[16]

Together with the manifesto, these principles reflect the people-centric nature of the new methodologies. Calling out a few of the principles, we can see that common practices provide a framework for transparency and curiosity in an Agile team:

- *Business people and developers must work together daily throughout the project:* Commonly embodied as a short daily meeting—and called a standup regardless of the actual posture of the participants—this is an opportunity for developers to transparently share both progress and obstacles, and to ask for support from others on the team as needed.

- *The best architectures, requirements, and designs emerge from self-organizing teams*: Agile teams are expected to collaborate openly, discussing the trade-offs across alternatives, with each member transparently sharing their professional judgement and being curious about the judgement of others. This can be witnessed in practices such as the Planning Game, where estimates are publicly shared (transparency) and the differences are used to spark conversations (curiosity) to uncover what influences differences in opinion.
- *At regular intervals, the team reflects on how to become more effective, then tunes and adjusts its behavior accordingly:* One of the signature Agile practices is the retrospective, an opportunity for team members to discuss their experiences, both as individuals and as a team. There is a wide range of retrospective activities, such as those captured in the book *Agile Retrospectives: Making Good Teams Great*, and they all rely on the ability and willingness of team members to transparently share their experiences, and the curiosity of the team to learn about the experiences of others on the team.

Perhaps the most dramatic change introduced by Agile development was not how people on the team related to one another, but how Agile practitioners embraced customer collaboration, as reflected in the first two principles: *"Our highest priority is to satisfy the customer through early and continuous delivery of valuable software"* and *"Welcome changing requirements, even late in development. Agile processes harness change for the customer's competitive advantage."* Together, these two principles enshrine transparency and curiosity as the core protocols of Agile development between the team and the customer. By delivering software frequently, the Agile team provides the customer a transparent view of their progress, and the team is curious about what the customer would value next, even if it means upsetting their plans.

Agile development has never been just one thing, one set of practices, and certainly not the Taylorist vision of one best way to do things imposed everywhere. What it provides is a set of values and guideposts to build a resilient organization that can adapt to the tumultuous world in which we live.* At the core, the Agile approach demands a culture that can support collaboration and learning—a culture that has created conversations between people who had no reason to talk to each other in the software factory. The success of Agile has opened the doors to radical thinking far beyond the software teams in which it incubated.

Why, then, do we now see, over and over again, "feature factories" operating in the same spirit as those software factories of the nineties while claiming to be Agile? In fact, only the visible artifacts and processes have changed; the mind-set and the conversations, and therefore the culture, are the same. Instead of mounds of documentation and two-year project plans, these teams are fed a steady stream of features to implement without any connection to the upstream customer needs or the downstream business impact. The software assembly line has been replaced by a sweatshop, with piecework assigned to each worker. The labels are different—requirements may come in the form of stories or acceptance criteria instead of a monolithic document; there may be a burndown chart in place of a Gantt chart—but the outcome is the same: disconnected development, barriers to collaboration, endless handoffs, painfully slow progress, and often wrong software at the end of it all.

Lean Software: Empower the Team

Stealing from Toyota

In 2003, just a couple of years after the Snowbird meeting gave rise to Agile software development through the Agile Manifesto, two deeply experienced programmers and software team leaders (who happened to be married to each other) brought ideas from Lean Manufacturing into Agile circles with their book *Lean Software Development: An Agile Toolki*t. Mary and Tom Poppendieck delved heavily into the Toyota Production System's just-in-time, waste-reducing manufacturing methods to find insights, and translated them for the software world.

---

* In fact, Alistair Cockburn and a number of his colleagues have begun coaching companies on adopting a methodology-agnostic approach that provides exactly these simple guidelines, called "Heart of Agile."

The Poppendiecks distilled the essence of Lean Software into a set of challenging principles:[17]

1. Eliminate Waste
2. Amplify Learning
3. Decide As Late As Possible
4. Deliver As Fast As Possible
5. Empower the Team
6. Build Integrity In
7. See the Whole

The Poppendiecks emphasized themes of optimization everywhere, rapid learning through frequent delivery, and system tuning and thinking. None of these themes are compatible with the software factory, and many build on the Agile principles that were already chipping away at the status quo when the Poppendiecks wrote their first book in 2003.

Soon, Lean thinking and practices began to spread. Lean software teams:

- *Draw value-stream maps*, just like their manufacturing colleagues, to locate inefficiencies (also known as *muda*, a Japanese word for waste).
- *Look for and eliminate bottlenecks in their processes*, from initial feature invention all the way to customer delivery and adoption.
- *Aim to limit work in progress*, so a QA team, for example, will accept only ten new features to test rather than building up a huge backlog of work it can't process.
- *Emphasize "pulling" features* from one process step to the next rather than "pushing" them; so a programmer might pause her coding if there is no one available to review her work, rather than continuing to build up more "inventory" of unreviewed, unreleasable code.

As more companies embraced Lean software principles, more Lean manufacturing ideas showed their utility, including the Theory of Constraints for managing bottlenecks and the Kanban method, which did away with even the lightweight timeboxing of "sprints" in favor of a direct application of pulling work to regulate flow. Always pushing to "see the whole," Lean software expanded to encompass operations in organizations of all sizes, from startups (as in Eric Ries's *The Lean Startup: How Today's Entrepreneurs Use Continuous*

Innovation to Create Radically Successful Businesses) to multinationals (as in *Lean Enterprise: How High Performance Organizations Innovate at Scale*).

Empowerment Is the Key

At first glance, unlike the Agile Manifesto, there is little explicitly in the Poppendiecks' principles or Lean practices that suggests we need to worry very much about messy, inconvenient people and their difficulties in communication. Looking at the principles, we see that all but the second (Amplify Learning) and fifth (Empower the Team) are about processes and efficiencies. It's easy to conclude that all we need is technical analysis of value stream maps and cold, calculated elimination of waste—and many adopters of Lean methods did exactly this, to their cost.

But as Mary and Tom Poppendieck say in *Lean Software Development*, "The foundation of human respect is to provide an environment where capable workers actively participate in running and improving their work areas and are able to fully use their capabilities."[18] Now that certainly sounds more like Cockburn's "non-linear, first-order components," i.e., people! And if we continue to look deeper, we see more connections to the fundamental, people-oriented values of transparency and curiosity:

- To eliminate waste, incorporate integrity, and work with the whole system, we will need to be transparent about where we have erred in creating inefficiencies and about how the system works (and doesn't work!) as a whole.
- To amplify learning and deliver quickly, we will have to be curious about what options we have to achieve our goals and perhaps even experiment with multiple options simultaneously (a classic Lean strategy for quick learning).
- And to empower the team, we will need to be transparent with them about what we are trying to achieve and where they can contribute, and we will need to encourage their curiosity about all aspects of our customers and our business.

In fact, the successful Lean software teams we have seen rely heavily on vigorous, candid, continuous communication, with direct customer feedback, information radiators (like build status indicators and big, visible business-relevant charts), and even Toyota-style Andon lights (personal red/green/amber indicators used by team members to announce widely that they are stuck or blocked). These tools and practices, grounded in transparency and curiosity, are used to spur productive conversations about continuous improvement.

The problem is that, as with Agile development, too many organizations adopt the practices without the underlying spirit. We have seen organizations with the Lean Six-Sigma Green Belt certifications pinned to cubicle walls but lacking the culture of collaboration and continuous improvement. In our experience, this is a symptom of executives who thought transformation was something that could be purchased, and then wonder why the value stream maps and pull systems lie discarded and unused.

DevOps: Operators Are People Too

Sysadmins Stand Up

By 2009, the time was ripe for the humanistic software movement to broaden, and none knew it better than Patrick Debois, a frustrated consultant and project manager in Belgium. He was annoyed because on project after project, he saw how the deep divide between the responsibilities of developers and system administrators was holding back progress. Though many development teams were undoing the negative legacy of the software factory, they continued the same old practices when interacting with the operators who deployed and ran their code—minimal communication, low trust, and avoidance of difficult conversations. And just as they had within development teams, those behaviors slowed progress and kept everyone from delivering the right working software. It was clear that Agile development needed to move downstream: "The operations team needs to be agile, and it needs to be integrated into the project."[19]

Patrick began trying to find others interested in what he called "Agile System Administration." There were few takers at first—at one conference, only two people showed up to a session on the new topic.[20] But there were others thinking the same way, notably John Allspaw and Paul Hammond, heads of operations and engineering respectively at Flickr. Their presentation "10+ Deploys Per Day: Dev and Ops Cooperation at Flickr," which called passionately for collaboration and trust between developers and operators, rapidly spread through Agile circles.[21] Patrick watched a livestream of their talk with increasing excitement and, soon thereafter, launched the first "DevOpsDays" conference in Ghent. The DevOps movement, armed with powerful values and technical tools, had been born.

Respect, Trust, and No Blame

There is no DevOps czar, and there was never a DevOps equivalent of Snowbird, so there is no definitive list of DevOps principles. But the seminal Flickr presentation is one of the clearest statements of goals for DevOps that we are aware of, and it's useful as a litmus test to gauge how teams that claim to be DevOps focused truly behave. The principles from the second half of that presentation are below (lightly edited to fit nicely into a list):

> ### DevOps Principles
>
> 1. Respect
>   a. Don't stereotype
>   b. Respect others' expertise, opinions, and responsibilities
>   c. Don't just say "No"
>   d. Don't hide things
> 2. Trust
>   a. Trust that everyone is doing their best for the business
>   b. Share runbooks and escalation plans
>   c. Provide knobs and levers
> 3. Healthy attitude about failure
>   a. Failure will happen
>   b. Develop your ability to respond to failure
>   c. Hold fire drills
> 4. Blame avoidance
>   a. No finger-pointing
>   b. Devs: remember that broken code wakes people up
>   c. Ops: provide constructive feedback on painful areas[22]

Notice how explicit Allspaw and Hammond are about the crucial elements of trust, respect, and collaboration; this is clearly a movement for people, not machines.

That's not to say that there aren't key DevOps technical and team practices. These include:

- *Cross-functional team*: Developers and operators work together in a single team rather than in separate groups with a handoff of completed code from one to the other.
- *Cattle, not pets*: For DevOps-focused teams, servers are not special snowflakes with individual identities and custom configurations but undifferentiated, identical, fungible machines that can be replaced at a moment's notice.
- *Infrastructure as code*: Instead of manually configuring servers, system admins write programs (in special-purpose languages provided by tools like Puppet, Chef, or Kubernetes) to set up and test their machines.
- *Automated deployment*: Once the server is running, system admins and developers write more code together to make deployment to that server a one-click operation. That deployment can be triggered by continuous integration tools, further tightening the link to developers and their work.
- *Sharing metrics*: A team operating with a DevOps mind-set will have engineers and system admins alike looking at system uptime, error rates, user logins, and many more indicators of operational health, and addressing any indicated problems together.

No More BOFH

In the 1980s, Simon Travaglia invented the ultimate sysadmin caricature for the online publication *The Register*.[23] The Bastard Operator from Hell (or BOFH) despised developers and users alike and made it his purpose to increase their misery without limit. Travaglia went overboard for comic effect, of course, but he touched on the deep suspicion and mistrust present between developers and system administrators in traditional organizations, with impenetrable separation between the teams.

Thus, it's no surprise that the DevOps principles and practices above are so clear in their demand for collaboration above all else: share your runbooks, display your metrics, discuss your failures (transparency). And respect the other "side" by avoiding finger-pointing and by finding out what effects your actions have (curiosity). By focusing on shared concerns and bringing developers and system administrators into a conversation with each other rather than about each other, DevOps moved away from the assembly-line mentality, with people-oriented values and attributes underpinning the DevOps movement—at least as it was originally conceived.

Bewilderingly, among some enterprises, there is a recent trend of anointing a special team that is separate from development and operations: the "DevOps" team. The whole point of DevOps is to create unity and collaboration among different specialties, not more silos. We even see job ads for "DevOps engineers," who apparently are a special breed different from normal engineers and system admins. What happened? We believe this is the result of a buzzword-bingo approach to management. Rather than cultivating "individuals and interactions," we have organizations hoping to avoid rethinking how to operate and instead get by with a reconfiguration of the software factory. And the surprising thing is that many have achieved that dubious goal.

Detour into the Feature Factory

The success of Agile development, Lean software, and DevOps in transforming the landscape of software is undeniable. Ideas that seemed extreme are considered normal now. Completing a feature in a day or an epic in a week is no longer astonishing, even in the largest corporations. As described by Eric Minick, program director at IBM,

> Looking at history, the most striking thing to me is that delivery has actually gotten better. Just look at release cadences. Teams were content with an annual release cycle. As agile hit corporations, they were then proud to get to quarterly. If you're at quarterly now, that's slower than average. Monthly is more normal now. Almost every big enterprise has some cloud-native team releasing daily or better. Today's cadence is an order of magnitude or two better than 15–20 years ago. Not bad.[24]

While a lot has changed in the schedules and the scope of our projects, there are times when we feel a sense of déjà vu. Large organizations are often stuck with a few Agile or Lean or DevOps processes uncomfortably coexisting with the old methods in a weird combination of practices—a "water-Scrum-fall" chimera.[25] And we've met many small organizations and startups where the practices from Lean, Agile, and DevOps are on display, yet the designers and developers and operations people describe themselves as working in a "feature factory," with all the same micromanagement and autonomy-destroying practices as before. It's as if the giant software factory has been reassembled using smaller pieces with different names. There have been real benefits, but this isn't the "enthusiasm, close collaborative teamwork, superb customer connection, and conscious design thinking" that inspired Richard Sheridan to write a book with the radical title *Joy, Inc.*[26] What happened?

One part of the answer comes from Niels Pflaeging, who tackled the question in his article "Why We Cannot Learn a Damn Thing from Toyota, or Semco." Pflaeging ponders why so many well-known examples of practices that work at pioneering organizations generate so little change. His insight is that what holds back transformations is the lack of "that magic ingredient . . . our image of human nature, the way we think about people around us, and what drives them."[27]*

Organizations have embraced the process and tools created by the Agile transformation, yet the Taylorist factory mind-set remains. There's a lot less documentation to write, fewer specifications to read, and hardly any mandated signoffs, but these practices have merely been replaced with endless planning meetings and many pages of tickets in a project management tool—practices that still offer the Taylorist promise of giving management the insight and control they demand, because the role of managers is still to ensure that the right things get done.

What about the people doing the work? Remember those nonlinear, first-order components of software development? They remain first order and they remain nonlinear. Cynthia Kurtz's and David Snowden's Cynefin framework (see the sidebar on page 20) gives us language to discuss them.[28] The feature factory wants to put humans in the lower-right, "obvious" quadrant: "If we have everyone in the planning meeting and the standup and the retrospectives, then they will collaborate." This cargo-cult approach to collaboration doesn't work with humans, whose nature is squarely in the upper-left, "complex" quadrant. Deliberately cultivating the dynamics of an effective organization takes a lot more work and a lot more skill than just putting a group of people cheek by jowl and calling them a team.

If we understand that the individuals and teams in our organizations are complex systems in and of themselves, then what should we do? According to the Cynefin framework, the appropriate way to navigate in complex scenarios,

---

* See "Preparing: Theory X and Theory Y" in Chapter 7 for more on this key ingredient.

where there are no guaranteed right answers, is to "probe-sense-respond."[29] So, how do we probe-sense-respond with humans? That's called a conversation—and it's the way out of the factory.

Sidebar: The Cynefin Framework

Cynefin is a *sense-making* framework whose goal is to allow shared understandings to emerge and to improve decision-making (see Figure 1.1).

Figure 1.1: The Cynefin Framework

While there are a rich set of activities and applications in the Cynefin community, the first lesson of the framework is that appropriate behavior depends on which domain you find yourself in.

- When the situation is Obvious (causes and their effects are well understood), tools such as flowcharts are useful, because there are a limited number of possibilities, and the current state determines the next right step.
- When the situation is Complicated (causes and effects are known but only to specialists), with intricate needs such as troubleshooting unexpected behavior in a sophisticated machine, you'll need

to develop the relevant knowledge, either through homegrown analysis or by bringing in an expert.

- When the situation is Complex (causes and effects are only understood retrospectively), with unpredictable parts such as evolving team dynamics over the course of a project, past experience in other contexts (other teams) is not a sufficient guide for what to do next; instead, you need to experiment and develop multiple perspectives to understand the patterns that exist before deciding how to respond.
- And in a Chaotic situation (with no link between causes and effects), such as an outage in a distributed system, it is appropriate to act first in an attempt to bring the situation into a state where the normal relationships between cause and effect again apply.

As a body of theory, Cynefin is relevant to software and humans several times over. The software systems we build are, at least, Complicated and often have (unplanned) Complex emergent behaviors. The teams building the software system are complex systems themselves. And Cynefin further recognizes that humans are complex in and of themselves, not bound by simple rules. The framework gives us a good language for describing why the mass-manufacturing approach to software, with simple jobs performed by supposedly interchangeable workers, had such disastrous results.

Chapter 2

Improving Your Conversations

This chapter will prepare you for the key relationship-building conversations you need in order to escape the feature factory: the Trust Conversation, the Fear Conversation, the Why Conversation, the Commitment Conversation, and the Accountability Conversation. Before you tackle the specific conversations, however, it is important to learn how to analyze and build your conversational skills generally. You will learn about why conversations are humanity's unique superpower and how to harness this power effectively through study and practice.

This chapter will also describe the core challenge to improving our conversations, which is that our behavior doesn't match our beliefs, and we are unaware of the gap. To combat this problem, we will provide a process to help you become aware: the Four Rs. We will show you how to Record your conversations, how to Reflect on them to find problems, how to Revise them to produce better alternatives, and how to Role Play to gain fluency. Finally, we will provide some sample conversations that will allow you to see the process in action.

Once you have the foundation of the Four Rs, you'll be ready for Part II of the book, where you will learn how to have each of the specific conversations.

Conversations: Humanity's Secret Weapon

Our Special Power

In his book *Sapiens: A Brief History of Humankind*, Yuval Noah Harari explores what has allowed humans to become the dominant species on the planet. His answer is that we have a special kind of communication, unique among animals.[1]

Many animals can communicate the idea "Run away from the lion!" through barks, chirps, or movement. Building on top of that, the development of human and animal communication seems to have been driven by the need to share information about others of the same species—the need to gossip. Gossiping allowed us, as social animals, to understand each other and have established reputations; and this, in turn, allowed us to collaborate in larger groups and to develop more sophisticated collaboration. In fact, understanding other humans, developing a "theory of mind," is so important that philosopher Daniel Dennett, in *From Bacteria to Bach and Back: The Evolution of Minds*, makes the case that our own consciousness arose as a byproduct of understanding the minds of others.[2]

Though our ability to gossip surpasses that of other species, Harari says that what is really unique about human language is our ability to discuss nonexistent things.[3] With this special power, we are able to create and believe shared fictions. These fictions allow us to collaborate at tremendous scales and across groups of people who have never met. In this way, a community's belief in a crocodile-headed god can create flood control works on the Nile, as described by Harari in another of his books, *Homo Deus: A Brief History of Tomorrow*.[4] And a shared belief in continuous improvement can allow us to create a learning environment and a performance-oriented culture rather than a power-oriented or rule-oriented culture, as described in *Accelerate: The Science of Lean Software and DevOps: Building and Scaling High Performing Technology Organizations* by Nicole Forsgren, Jez Humble, and Gene Kim.[5]

Why Our Power Is Flawed

Conversation makes collaboration possible but not inevitable. We don't live in a world of universal acceptance, peace, and understanding. Earnest and well-intentioned people can disagree, and even come to view another person as an enemy, as "the other." Along with our amazing powers of conversation, we also come equipped with pre-existing, built-in flaws—our so-called cognitive biases (see Table 2.1 for a sampling of our favorite biases, and Daniel Kahneman, *Thinking, Fast and Slow*, for many more). These are biases that seem to be built into the functioning of our brains. And these cognitive biases inhibit the sort of collaboration our language makes possible

Name	Distortion
Egocentric bias	Give self undue credit for positive outcomes
False consensus effect	Believe that personal views are commonly held
Gambler's fallacy	Believe that a random event is influenced by previous outcomes
Illusion of control	Overestimate control over external events
Loss aversion	Value keeping a possession over gaining something of greater value
Naïve realism	Believe personal view of reality is accurate and without bias
Negativity bias	Recall unpleasant events more readily than positive ones
Normalcy bias	Refuse to plan for a novel catastrophe
Outcome bias	Judge decisions by their results instead of by the quality of the decision-making process

Table 2.1: A Sampling of Cognitive Biases

Our cognitive biases pose a threat to any adoption of Agile, Lean, or DevOps methods because they can seriously damage collaboration, relationships, and team productivity.

In the previous sections, we described how transparency and curiosity are woven into the fabric of people-centric practices, but these are undermined by a host of cognitive biases. An example is the false-consensus effect, where we believe our own views to be commonly held. This bias makes us less likely to either share our reasoning or to ask about the reasoning of others. What's the point when we believe we already agree? Naïve realism, the belief that we see reality as it is, without bias, is yet more corrosive to team dynamics in that we see any disagreement as a sign that the other party is uninformed, irrational, lazy, biased, or perhaps all of those! Under the influence of these and other cognitive biases, Agile, Lean, and DevOps practices can fail to deliver the promised benefits.

Learning from Conversations

Conversations as an Investigative Tool

Social scientist Chris Argyris studied organizational behavior, particularly in businesses, in a long and illustrious academic career at the business schools of Yale and Harvard. His areas of research included individual and organizational learning, and effective interventions that "promote learning at the level of norms and values."[6] The humble conversation was the central tool Argyris used for investigating group effectiveness and for improving organizational performance. What Argyris found was that conversations, together with the unexpressed thoughts of the participants in those conversations, revealed everything he needed to know about the "theories of action" of the people and organizations he studied.

Argyris and collaborator Donald Schön use the term "theory of action" to describe the logic—the "master program"—behind our actions.[7] According to Argyris and Schön, we all have outcomes we want to achieve, and we use our theory of action to choose which steps to take. If my theory of action has a focus on learning, then I will take actions that generate information, like sharing everything I know that is relevant to the situation and asking others about what they know. If my theory of action is centered on getting my own way, then I will only share information that supports my position, and I won't ask questions to which I don't know the answer.

In general we don't explicitly think about our theories of action; however, as with the two examples we just provided, we can understand them after the fact by examining our choice of action. One of the findings of Argyris and Schön is that there is often a gap between what we say we would do in a situation (espoused theory) and what we actually do (theory in use).[8]

Defensive versus Productive Reasoning: What We Do and What We Say We Do

Before reading on, consider this question: If you had an important choice to make as a group, how would you recommend the group go about making the decision?

When we ask this question of our audiences, we get remarkably consistent answers. The typical response is something like, "I'd have everyone share all the information they have, explain their ideas and reasoning, and then see if we can agree on the best way to proceed."

If your answer sounded like this, congratulations! You have espoused what Argyris and his colleagues call the Model II Theory of Action,[9] or "productive reasoning."[10] You claim to value transparency, sharing your reasoning and information. You also claim to value curiosity, hearing everyone's thoughts to learn their reasoning and what information they have that you don't. Finally, you claim to value collaboration and jointly designing how to proceed. While you might have used different words, these are commonly understood and accepted practices to increase learning and make better decisions. In fact, you likely *do* behave this way in nonthreatening situations, where nothing important is at stake. Unfortunately, if you are like the more than 10,000 people that Argyris studied across all ages and cultures[11] (and those we've met!), *your behavior won't match your words* when the topic is something important—like introducing a company strategy or leading a cultural transformation.

Argyris and colleagues found that although almost everyone claims to adopt the approaches and behaviors of productive reasoning, things change when the situation is potentially threatening or embarrassing. In those cases, what people *actually* do closely matches a very different theory-in-use that Argyris terms the Model I Theory of Action, or "defensive reasoning."[12]

We contrast these two theories of action in Table 2.2. When using a defensive reasoning mind-set, people act to remove the threat or potential embarrassment. To do so, they tend to act unilaterally and without sharing their reasoning, they think in terms of winning and losing, they avoid expressing negative feelings, and they attempt to be seen as acting rationally.

	Model I	Model II
Governing Values	Define and achieve the goal Win; do not lose Suppress negative feelings Be rational	Valid information Free and informed choice Internal commitment
Strategies	Act unilaterally Own the task Protect self Unilaterally protect others	Share control Design tasks jointly Test theories publicly
Useful When...	Data is easily observed Situation is well understood	Data is conflicting or hidden Situation is complex

Based on Argyris, Putnam, and McLain Smith[13]

Table 2.2: Model I and Model II Theories of Action Compared

This gap between our espoused theory and our theory-in-use gets at the heart of a paradox of team productivity. In theory, we value diverse teams because we understand that diversity can be a strength. A diversity of experiences, a diversity of knowledge, and even a diversity of modes of thought—in theory, these all make a team stronger, because every new element gives the team more information and more ideas, and therefore, more options to make better choices.

What we should be seeking from our diversity is *productive conflict*, through which we harness our differences to create new ideas and better options. In practice, we tend to see differences of opinion as threatening and potentially embarrassing, so we react defensively. Our defensive reasoning leads us to suppress the diversity we claimed to value and to avoid the productive exchange of ideas that we claimed to seek!

What does this defensive reasoning look like in practice? We will illustrate many flavors of defensive reasoning with examples throughout the book, but to paraphrase Tolstoy's *Anna Karenina*, each productive conversation is alike, and each defensive conversation is defensive in its own way. That said, there are common elements; and defensive reasoning in conversations will tend to feature hidden motives, undiscussable issues, and reacting to, rather than relating to, what is said—all characteristics that inhibit learning and corrode relationships.

Transforming Conversations

So, why do people choose these counterproductive, defensive behaviors rather than the behaviors we all agree would produce better results? The answer is that we don't consciously choose. In everyday activities, this gap between the theories we espouse and the theories we use is invisible to us. We effortlessly produce the defensive behavior through years of practice—so effortlessly, in fact, that we aren't aware of what we are doing, no matter how counterproductive it is for us or how much it contradicts our espoused theory of productive reasoning. Even worse, we are so unaware of our defensive reasoning that we will deny we are acting defensively if someone else tries to bring it to our attention.

The good news is that Argyris found that reflecting on conversations allowed participants to become aware of and then change their behavior.[14] Through regular effort and practice, you can learn the behaviors of transparency and curiosity that will promote joint design and learning; the sharing of knowledge across organizational boundaries; and the sharing of and resolution of difficult, previously taboo issues. The bad news is that this takes substantial effort, and worse, this effort involves difficult emotional work.

The difficulty comes because it requires recognizing that your behaviors are contributing to the problem. Are you willing to consider that you might be contributing to unproductive meetings and defensive relationships? This is not a price everyone is willing to pay. Finally, even if you are willing to be humble and put in the effort, developing these new skills takes time. Argyris and colleagues describe overcoming our routine behaviors as taking about as much practice "as to play a not-so-decent game of tennis."[15] If this seems daunting, it may help to remember that you get the opportunity to practice every day as you work to solve real problems in your organization. We can give you the skills to practice if you have the drive to improve.

Later in this chapter, we will show you how to practice productive reasoning by learning from the conversations you are having today. In addition to providing the core technique for learning from conversations (the Four Rs), we will provide examples for you to practice your analysis. Through the remainder of the book, you'll be using this same Four Rs approach again and again to learn the specifics of the Trust, Fear, Why, Commitment, and Accountability Conversations. These five conversations address the common pitfalls that prevent us from using the productive reasoning we espouse. These pitfalls are:

1. We won't be transparent and curious when we lack **Trust**.
2. We will, consciously or not, act defensively when we have unspoken **Fear**.
3. We will be unable to generate productive conflict when we lack a shared **Why**.
4. We will avoid definite **Commitments** as long as the situation feels threatening or embarrassing.
5. We will fail to learn from our experiences if we are unwilling to be **Accountable**.

It is only after we have overcome each of these challenges that we can really have the productive learning conversations required for a high-performing organization.

Sidebar: Types of Conversations

From cover to cover, this book is about conversations, so it is worth taking a moment to explain the range of conversation types where this material is applicable.

The first image that comes to mind when we say "conversation" is probably a face-to-face encounter with two or more people in the same room. However, most of us have a number of other types of communication channels we use regularly. Email is ubiquitous. Chat systems such as Slack, Microsoft Teams, and IRC (internet relay chat) are being adopted right and left. Distributed meetings with video are increasingly common, a big step up from the voice-only conference call.

We believe the material in this book is useful across all these conversation modes, though it is worth considering the trade-offs inherent in the different options. Figure 2.1 provides a useful visual reference for these trade-offs based on a model by Alistair Cockburn.[16]

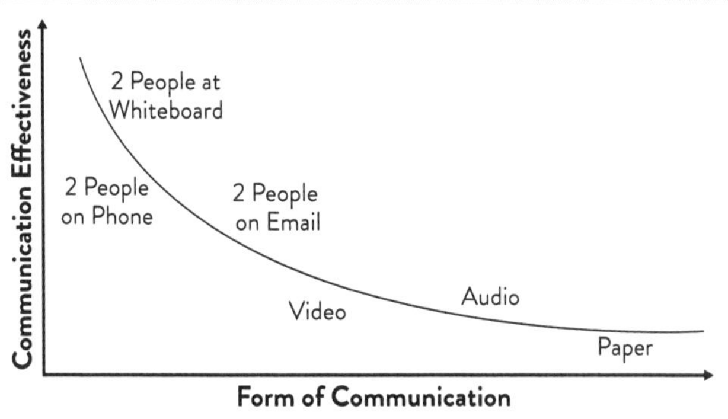

Figure 2.1: Effectiveness of Different Modes of Communication

As Cockburn says, "the most effective communication is person-to-person, face-to-face, as with two people at the whiteboard."[17] This scenario is the most effective, because, among other attributes, it offers the maximum possible nonverbal information to the two participants, and the fastest response rate. However, these same attributes can make it more difficult when you are learning to have difficult conversations and one or both parties are feeling strong emotions. A red face is additional information, but it can also be intimidating and distracting.

As an opportunity for learning, asynchronous channels can offer some benefits. One is that you'll likely have a better record of what each party actually said, which can be a big help in performing a later conversational analysis.* Even better, an asynchronous channel allows us to make multiple drafts before responding. As an example, we've applied the Four Rs to draft emails, allowing

* Recording video of your face-to-face conversations at the whiteboard for later review is a great practice that we'd recommend, though it's underused in most teams we've worked with.

us to use a technique we are learning and to incorporate the insights into the email we finally sent.

Ultimately the skill you are after is the ability to apply these techniques face to face and in real time; making good use of the learning opportunities of asynchronous communication can help you gain that ability.

The Four Rs

Experiences give us the *opportunity* to learn, but most people don't take the time to actually learn from them. We apply the Four Rs—Record, Reflect, Revise, and Role Play—as our preferred way of learning from conversations. (As you can see in Figure 2.2, there are two additional Rs that can sneak in along the way: Repeat and Role Reversal.)

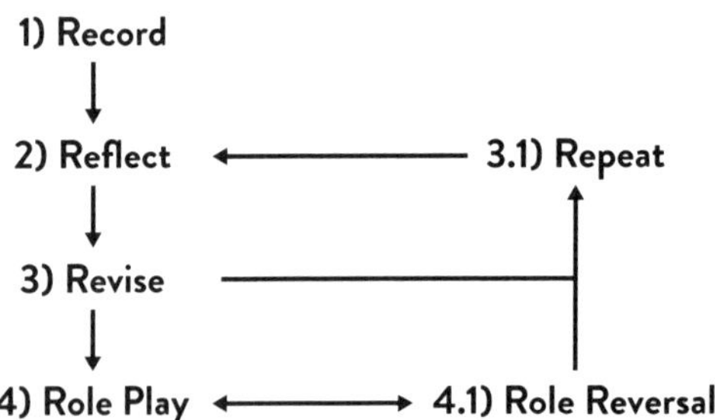

Figure 2.2: The Four Rs

To start using the Four Rs, you will need to Record a conversation in writing. In the next section, we describe our preferred method for this, the Two-Column Conversational Analysis. It may be tempting to avoid pen and paper and just think about the conversation "in your mind's eye," or talk about it with a friend. *Do not do this!* The act of writing down the words on paper is an inherent part of the process because it forces your brain to think about the conversation at arm's length, as if it were happening to someone else. This distance is vital to gaining insights through reflection and revision, as we'll see later.*

After you have Recorded the conversation, it's time to Reflect on it, paying attention to the tool or technique you are trying to use at the time. For each of the Five Conversations, we will suggest particular tools. With time and practice, you will move between them as the conversation requires, but to start with, we recommend you use one tool or technique at a time. We will give you guidelines on how to score your conversation using the tool, and that reflection will lead you to possible improvements.

Having scored the conversation, Revise your conversation to try and produce a better result. How will you know if you've improved? Repeat: take your revised dialogue and Reflect again. Did you improve your score from the first time around? You may be surprised to find that your revised version in fact shows no better scores than your original! Don't be discouraged—this is very common, especially as you are learning a new skill. It might take you half a dozen or more attempts to produce a revision that checks all the boxes of the technique.

Having created the dialogue for an alternative conversation, there's still an important step remaining: Role Play. Find a friend who is willing to help, and try saying your dialogue aloud, with your friend taking the part of your conversation partner. How does it feel to say the words out loud? Often what seems okay in writing feels unnatural coming out of your mouth. Perhaps the words need to change, or perhaps you just need practice talking in a different way.

Another good check on your progress is the other hidden R: Role Reversal. Trade places in your dialogue and have your friend say your words. How does it feel to be in the other person's shoes and to hear your revised language? Frequently, hearing your own words will give you clues as to how you can further tune the dialogue to feel more natural while keeping in place the skills you are trying to practice.

Following all of the Four Rs for a single conversation will offer the most learning from that single experience. Following them for a series of conversations will dramatically increase the volume and pace of your learning overall, and should quickly give you and your team substantial practical gains.

---

* An extreme version of this distancing was practiced by our friend and teacher Benjamin Mitchell, who used an audio recorder to capture his conversations. He tells us that when he first listened to himself on tape, when he noticed mistakes he was making, he would shout at the recorder, "Benjamin! Don't do that!"

Conversational Analysis

The first step of the Four Rs is, as we just explained, is to Record the conversations you want to improve. We're about to show you a remarkable technique invented and used by Chris Argyris for capturing the key elements of a conversation. We particularly like this method for two reasons: first, it is clearly specified and mechanical, which appeals to our engineering brains; and second, it very naturally lends itself to the other three Rs: Reflect, Revise, and Role Play.

At first, conversational analysis may seem too simple to be valuable. But it is the fastest route to gaining significant insights and improved conversations. We use it throughout the book to illustrate how to make each of the Five Conversations successful.

You Will Need

1. A single sheet of ordinary writing paper (*Don't* get more than a single sheet, for a reason we'll explain shortly.).
2. A pen, pencil, or other writing implement.

That's it, really. (We told you it was simple!) Again, don't let yourself skip the task of writing by saying you'll imagine or remember the content—write it down on a real piece of paper. You'll be glad you did when your distance helps you with a crucial insight.

Step 1: Record Your Conversation

Think of a conversation you would like to improve. This can be one you had recently, but it doesn't have to be: you can analyze a conversation that occurred long ago or (this is a favorite of ours) one that hasn't happened yet that you're worried about.

Next, fold the paper down the middle the long way, creating two columns. In the right-hand column, write down what each person in the conversation said. Don't worry about getting every word right; you're aiming for the sound and flavor of the conversation, not exact quotes. On the other hand, try hard not to editorialize or add anything to the words. You're trying to record what a neutral listener or mechanical audio recorder would hear.

In the left-hand column, after you have written the dialogue, write what you thought at the time as the words were spoken. Don't hold back here; often in a difficult conversation, your thoughts will be very different from what you said, so include everything that crossed your mind, no matter how irrelevant or unfair it may seem. *Important warning*: you must *not* write anything that the other person thought.*

Tip: Keep It Short

We find that newcomers to the conversational analysis method often write far more than they need to, trying to capture every word of what might be a lengthy conversation. This is almost certainly unnecessary. If you concentrate on the most emotionally charged part of the conversation for you, it is very likely that you will be able to fit that key section onto just one side of your piece of paper, which is exactly why we told you to prepare only one sheet.

Keeping the case very focused like this probably means that you'll need to start in the middle of the conversation rather than at the beginning. Don't worry about this; it's safe to assume that the reader knows the context of the conversation and what the participants said earlier, since the chief reader is going to be you!

If you find it hard to keep your case this short, try making it even shorter, just half the page.† The restriction to a very limited length will help you create a more valuable, analysis-friendly case.

An Example Two-Column Conversational Analysis

Let's look at a real conversation between the authors using the two-column analysis technique. This example concisely illustrates all the key characteristics of a conversational analysis: it's short, the thoughts and the actual words are

---

* There are two exceptions: First, you may include the other person's thoughts if you write the case jointly with them—this can be a very rewarding exercise, as well as a terrifying one (see Chapter 5 for an example). Second, the rule does not apply to you if you have developed telepathy. But if you can really read minds, then frankly, most of this book will not be of much use to you!

† We have recently had success with even shorter "two row" cases, containing just one sentence by you and one by the other person. Key insights can still be found even in very short exchanges, we assure you!

both included, and there are rich opportunities for learning by looking at the differences between the two columns.

When you read someone else's recorded conversation, read the columns in the order they are recorded: read the right column first so that you understand the spoken dialogue, then go back and read the columns together so that you understand the inner dialogue that is happening along with the outer one. If you just jump in and read left to right and top to bottom, as is natural in English, you will hear that Squirrel is concerned about Jeffrey's absence before Jeffrey announces that he'll be away. If you're reading out loud, you might add a reminder of the distinction between thoughts and speech: "Jeffrey says, 'I'll be out of the country for our next scheduled online training.'" Squirrel thinks, *Ouch! Jeffrey usually sets up the phone and software connection*, and so on. We aren't usually aware of the distinction between the inner and outer dialogue, which makes this format helpful but sometimes tricky to grasp at first. Be patient: analyses become much easier to follow after you've recorded your own conversations a few times.

Jeffrey and Squirrel's Conversation

What Squirrel thought and felt	What Jeffrey and Squirrel said
Ouch! Jeffrey usually sets up the phone and software connection. What do we do now?	Jeffrey: I'll be out of the country for our next scheduled online training.
Seems doomed. I think we'll just have to give up.	Squirrel: Okay, that means we can't do it at your office, I guess. Should we cancel?
Sure, but how will I get the technology to work? It always seems fiddly when Jeffrey does it.	Jeffrey: Oh no, I'm sure I can dial in. Then you can stay at home and won't have to come to the office.
That's a good point—I'll save on the commute stress.	Squirrel: Yes, I guess you can join on the phone, and that would mean less travel for me. But I've never done the software and phone setup.

I'm far less confident than Jeffrey is about this.	Jeffrey: Don't worry. The organizer sent us a link to a very helpful tutorial. You won't have any trouble.
What will I do if I screw it up? Hundreds of attendees will be furious with me for delaying the session they've paid for. I suppose I'll just have to give it a go.	Squirrel: Well, I guess I can give it a try.

If you read just the right-hand column, you see a relatively calm conversation, with Squirrel expressing only mild doubts. That is indeed what you would have observed if you'd been in the room with us. But the left-hand column reveals far more about Squirrel's inner fears and worries, with words like "doomed" and "furious" illustrating his depth of feeling. These unexpressed and perhaps undiscussable thoughts and feelings are exactly what we are going to concentrate on when we analyze cases using the techniques we are about to show you.

Analyzing a Conversation: Reflect, Revise, and Role Play

Once you have your conversation down on paper, it's time to take it apart, understand how it works, and look for ways to improve it—the Reflect, Revise, and Role Play steps of the Four Rs. As you are critiquing your conversation, you'll want to test yourself against standards. We suggest examining conversations for evidence of transparency and curiosity, as these are fundamental elements of collaboration. Also attempt to notice patterns of behavior that apply across conversations.

As we Reflect on the conversation, we will be marking up the dialogue to help guide our later revision (see Figure 2.3 on page 44). Consider changing to a red pen (or other color) to make your markings obvious.

We're going to start with a conversation analyzed by Norbert, a system administrator for a midsize organization. He and his boss, Quinn, are trying to decide which virtualization software will be the best to use in a new project.

Norbert and Quinn's Actual Conversation

Reminder: read the right-hand column first, then go back and read right to left.

What Norbert thought and felt	What Norbert and Quinn said
Open source is obviously the way to go.	Norbert: I think we should go with KVM here. It's the most flexible and fits our needs best.
Only if you count "waiting on hold for support" as an efficient use of my time.	Quinn: It's not our standard, though. Virt-App is working efficiently on all our existing projects.
Why are you always pushing closed-source solutions?	Norbert: Okay, but we wait for fixes from them all the time, and it's awful. Wouldn't you rather be in control, so we can address problems ourselves?
Nonsense! They all know KVM already, at least the basics.	Quinn: Yes, but think about the retraining costs. I don't think I could get additional budget for everyone to learn a new tool.
Not much training needed in fact—everyone's already using it on their side projects.	Norbert: Why don't we ask the team? I'm sure they'd be willing to self-train.
Weren't you just saying you wanted us to have more autonomy?? What a hypocrite you are!	Quinn: Unfortunately I can't leave budget-critical decisions like this up to the team.
Typical manager, not willing to take any risks. There's no point arguing against a decision that you've already made.	Norbert: Okay, but I think you're missing a real opportunity here.

"I wasn't too pleased with this conversation," Norbert said afterward. "Quinn shot down my preferred solution, and what's worse, I felt I was manipulated into agreeing to use Virt-App, Quinn's favorite." We can see this negative view developing in the left-hand column of Norbert's conversation record, which starts with sarcasm and ends with fatalism.

How could Norbert have changed this conversation to achieve a different result? Below, we describe how he analyzed the conversation to discover more effective options. These are basic analysis steps you can use with any conversation. As you learn more techniques throughout the book, we'll suggest further ways to score and learn from conversations, where you are employing a particular technique.

Reflect on Curiosity: The Question Fraction

The first principle of productive reasoning we are looking for is curiosity; and to assess how curious we are being, we start with the Question Fraction. To find the Question Fraction for this conversation, Norbert first looked at his right-hand column and circled all the question marks, finding two. He wrote this down at the top of the right-hand column as the bottom half of a fraction: $\frac{?}{2}$.

Now the hard part: Norbert asked himself, "Were each of my questions genuine?" A *genuine question* has these characteristics:[18]

- You really want to know the answer.
- It's reasonable to expect that the answer might surprise you.
- You are willing to change your views or behavior as a result of the answer you get.

By contrast, nongenuine questions are used to make a point rather than learn something new. They are often statements in disguise, or attempts to *lead* the other person to a conclusion. Lawyers are particularly good at leading questions, designed to force specific answers out of an unwilling witness: "Did you drive to Bob's house at noon? The neighbors saw you pounding on the door and shouting angrily, isn't that right? And when he answered the door, you pulled out your gun, didn't you?"

Crucially, you can't distinguish between genuine and nongenuine questions simply by listening to them. The same words may be genuine in one context and nongenuine in another. The key to the distinction is the thoughts, often unexpressed, of the person asking the question. For example, if I ask you, "Have you fixed that critical bug yet?" I may genuinely want to know the status of the fix, or I may be trying to pressure you to work on it, or I may be subtly complaining that you haven't started on a feature that I view as of the highest importance. Only my left-hand column (my thoughts) will reveal my true motives.

Reflecting on the genuineness of his questions, Norbert said, "It's hard to admit, but I can see from my left-hand column that neither of my questions were genuine. I asked the first one, about being in control, because I wanted to push Quinn to use open source. And when I suggested we ask the team, I was leading the witness—I knew they would favor KVM, and this was a way to get more evidence on my side."

Since none of his questions were genuine, Norbert places a zero in the numerator of his fraction: $\frac{0}{2}$. "Wow, I guess it is obvious I wasn't very curious about what Quinn was thinking. I didn't ask a single genuine question."

To reiterate, as you analyze your conversation, add up the number of questions you asked; this is your denominator. Then analyze how many of your questions were genuine; this is your numerator:

$$\frac{\textbf{Genuine Questions}}{\textbf{Questions Asked}}.$$

The Question Fraction helps you understand how much curiosity you are demonstrating in your conversation. You might believe you held the conversation with an open mind, but if you weren't asking genuine questions, you weren't demonstrating that curiosity. This will be valuable input as you move on to the Revise step.

Reflect on Transparency: Unexpressed Thoughts and Feelings

Next, Norbert turned to his left-hand column. As is usual in difficult conversations, this column has many statements and questions that do *not* appear in the right-hand column; in other words, it contains unshared ideas that represent unexpressed thoughts and feelings.

Emotions are particularly difficult for people to share in conversations. Not only do we lack practice in doing so but talking about emotions also violates two of the standard principles of the defensive mind-set: avoid expression of negative feelings and be seen as acting rationally.

When reflecting on how we can productively share our emotions, it is worth considering Marshall Rosenberg's guidelines for sharing feelings from his book *Nonviolent Communication: A Language of Life*:[19]

- Distinguish feelings from thoughts. We often say "I feel" followed by a thought, as in "I feel like we made the wrong choice." If we can substitute "I feel" with "I think," then we aren't expressing an emotion.
- Distinguish between what we feel and what we think we are. "I feel like a fraud" is sharing a thought about what we think we are, not an emotion.
- Distinguish between what we feel and how we think others react or behave toward us. This is perhaps the most difficult of these guidelines to apply, because when we say "I feel ignored" or "misunderstood" or something similar, we are actually making a statement about other people—that they are ignoring or misunderstanding us. We are not sharing an emotion.
- Build a vocabulary for feelings. Saying "I felt good when that happened" isn't very specific, nor is "I felt bad when that happened." English has dozens of words to describe specific emotional states. (See the handy "Feelings Inventory" from the Center for Nonviolent Communication.[20]) Spend the effort to find the one that most accurately expresses how you feel.

What makes these guidelines difficult is that these statements, though not expressions of emotion directly, all raise strong emotions in us. Because the emotions are strong and clear to us, we assume they are obvious to others as well. This cognitive bias, known as the "Illusion of Transparency," is one of the barriers to genuine transparency. Why should we share something that is obvious? As we reflect on our conversations, it is important to remember that if we aren't explicitly sharing our emotions, then we aren't being transparent.

When we review our unshared thoughts, it is also worth remembering another tip from Rosenberg: distinguish evaluations from observations.[21] It is in our nature to instantly and effortlessly assign an intent to the actions we see from other people, as when Norbert brands Quinn as a "hypocrite." These evaluations arise so quickly, it is easy to mistake them for the truth. Similarly, we read emotions into other people and are inappropriately confident of our judgement (the Illusion of Transparency again). When we notice these attributions of intent, or emotions that haven't been stated by the other person, they should be a trigger for curiosity—a trigger for us to inquire how the other person is actually thinking and feeling.

With all of this in mind, Norbert underlined each sentence in the left-hand column (his thoughts) that was *not* expressed, even partially, in the right-hand column.

"I gave myself the benefit of the doubt in the first two rows," said Norbert. "I did indirectly express support for open source further along in the dialogue, and I did mention waiting when explaining my opposition to Virt-App, though I didn't quite say how passionately I hated wasting my time on hold with them. My thoughts became increasingly negative and dismissive in the following rows, and I didn't share any of those feelings, so I underlined everything else. Looking at everything I underlined, I can see I wasn't very transparent with Quinn. I didn't share all the facts that I had, and I didn't share *any* of the emotions I was feeling at the time."

Reflect on Patterns: Triggers, Tells, and Twitches

Now Norbert looked for his individual *triggers*, *tells*, and *twitches* in the dialogue. These are personal and, as such, will tend to become apparent when you've analyzed several of your conversations and notice repeating patterns of behavior.

- A *trigger* is a behavior, statement, or other event outside yourself that typically causes you to react strongly. For instance, a less-experienced developer might become depressed and withdraw from the conversation when he hears the term "junior engineer" applied to him, as this makes him feel less valuable to the team.
- A *tell* (like in poker) is a behavior you exhibit that signals you are not acting with transparency and curiosity. For example, a manager might begin to pace around the meeting room when he's frustrated and believes his team isn't accepting his direction.
- A *twitch* is your instinctive default response, regardless of the details of the situation. For instance, one person may have a bias to get to a decision quickly and adjust later, while another might have a bias toward delaying a decision until all the facts are in.

Learning your triggers, tells, and twitches can help you become more self-aware and give you more choices in how you respond in the moment. We have both benefited from this type of analysis ourselves. Squirrel discovered a trigger by noticing he felt anxious and defensive when a very tall person he was working with would stand over him; he adjusted by standing up when talking with tall colleagues. Jeffrey learned from analyzing his conversations that he would say "obviously" and raise his left hand just before describing something that wasn't obvious; now, when Jeffrey catches himself doing this, he says, "It isn't obvious," and then explains what he's thinking.

No twitch is wrong; however, no twitch is right in all situations either. When you notice yourself acting in line with your twitch, it can be a useful prompt to consider whether that twitch is a good fit for the scenario of the moment.

"I found one trigger and one tell in this dialogue," said Norbert. "First, I reacted really strongly to Quinn's refusal to consult the team, calling him a hypocrite in my left-hand column. I often do this when people flatly refuse what seems like a reasonable request, so it's a trigger.

"Also, I used 'okay' twice, when I definitely wasn't feeling okay at all. The second time I was blasting Quinn in my left-hand column while agreeing with him in my right-hand column. I want to watch out for this tell in the future by noticing when I say 'okay' but don't feel that way."

When you identify a trigger, tell, or twitch in your conversation, circle the location and label it. Labeling it in the dialogue will help guide you through the Revise step, and it will also help you to recall it later, both in conversations and in future analysis.

Revise: Creating a Better Alternative

Finally it was time for Norbert to rewrite the dialogue in a way that addressed the issues he'd identified, using his annotated conversation record as a guide.

"I wanted to be more curious and to use more genuine questions," said Norbert. "And I also thought I should be more transparent by moving some of my challenging thoughts and feelings from the left-hand column to the right, phrasing them in a constructive way. And I wanted to design preplanned actions in response to the trigger and the tell that I'd identified. My goals were to practice the new skills I've learned, to discover more about Quinn's thinking, and to ensure Quinn heard just how much his management style grates on me."

What Norbert thought and felt	What Norbert and Quinn said
Open-source is obviously the way to go.	Norbert: I think we should go with KVM here. It's the most flexible and fits our needs best. 0/2
Only if you count "waiting on hold for support" as an efficient use of my time.	Quinn: It's not our standard, though. Virt-App is working efficiently on all our existing projects.
Why are you always pushing closed-source solutions?	Tell — Norbert: Okay, but we wait for fixes from them all the time, and it's awful. Wouldn't you rather be in control, so we can address problems ourselves?
Nonsense! They all know KVM already, at least the basics.	Quinn: Yes, but think about the retraining costs. I don't think I could get additional budget for everyone to learn a new tool.
Not much training needed in fact—everyone's already using it on their side projects.	Norbert: Why don't we ask the team? I'm sure they'd be willing to self-train.
Weren't you just saying you wanted us to have more autonomy?? What a hypocrite you are!	Trigger! — Quinn: Unfortunately I can't leave budget-critical decisions like this up to the team.
Typical manager, not willing to take any risks. There's no point arguing against a decision that you've already made.	Tell — Norbert: Okay, but I think you're missing a real opportunity here.

Figure 2.3: Norbert's Annotated Conversation

Here's how Norbert revised his case:

Norbert and Quinn's Revised Discussion

What Norbert thought and felt	What Norbert and Quinn said
Open source seems like the way to go, but I'd also like to hear Quinn's ideas.	Norbert: I think we should go with KVM here because it's so flexible. What do you think?
That's a challenging answer. I don't count "waiting on hold for support" as an efficient use of my time!	Quinn: It sure is flexible but isn't our standard. Virt-App is working efficiently on all our existing projects.
Caught my tell! Does Quinn agree that we're overdependent on vendors?	Norbert: Okay—well, actually, it's not okay, because Virt-App is so inefficient at responding to our requests. I feel really frustrated by the amount of time I spend on hold for their support. I also worry about our level of vendor dependence; does it concern you?
Training is something to think about, but we have this covered.	Quinn: That's a good point. I didn't know about their poor response time. But what about the retraining costs? I don't think I could get additional budget for everyone to learn a new tool.
Not much training needed in fact—everyone's already using it on their side projects.	Norbert: Actually, almost everyone already knows KVM. I can check with them to be sure. Do you think that's a good next step?
Weren't you just saying you wanted us to have more autonomy?? This is one of my triggers, so I'll try raising the issue of autonomy directly.	Quinn: It's certainly good to get the information. But don't let them think the choice has been made; unfortunately, I can't leave budget-critical decisions like this up to the team.
I'm hopeful that we can have a meaningful discussion about increasing self-organization.	Norbert: You know, that doesn't sit well with me, because I think we need more autonomy, not less. Can we talk more about how we make decisions?

"This is by no means a perfect conversation," Norbert said, reflecting on his revisions. "But I managed to share most of my left-hand-column concerns. I also asked three genuine questions, and I caught my trigger and tell signals."

Try rescoring this second case yourself with the Question Fraction tool or by underlining for transparency and twitches, tells, and triggers, to see if you agree with Norbert that it's more effective. When you try this yourself, expect the reflection and revisions to be difficult at first, as the skills you are learning are easy to describe but hard to master. In fact it is quite normal to revise the same case multiple times, reflecting on the revisions and rescoring them. It can take several iterations to come up with a satisfactory alternative.

Role Play: Practice Producing a Better Conversation

Role Playing—the fourth of the Four Rs—helps a lot in making these new skills feel natural, so try reading out your revised dialogue with a friend, colleague, or even the mirror. When you speak the lines, consider how it feels to say them, and adjust the dialogue until it feels natural and comfortable. As a final test, reverse the roles with your friend and consider how it feels to hear those words spoken to you. Our experience is that people gain different insights and make different adjustments in each of these steps: writing, speaking, and listening.

"It was a lot harder than I expected to say the dialogue out loud," reflected Norbert. "Even in the role play, I could feel myself getting angry at the idea that the team couldn't be part of this kind of decision. And when we did the role reversal and I heard the dialogue played back to me, I realized that I didn't really share how frustrated I've been with the current situation. I made a final revision to share my feelings explicitly, and that sounded much more effective."

Example Conversation

You can practice your conversation analysis with the following example. Try scoring as we described above, and then rewrite the conversation to address the issues revealed by the scores. Don't worry if you find this difficult—everyone does at first, and there will be plenty of techniques to try and chances to practice throughout the rest of the book. We'll walk you through this first example.

Tanya and Kay: Limiting Work in Progress

Tanya says, "I just took a Lean Startup course and drew a value stream map for our Agile software team, where I'm the product owner. I think we need to start limiting our work in progress (WIP) because we have significant buffering at several steps in our development process. One big obstacle is that we're always waiting for Kay, our tester, to verify the latest changes before we release. I'm sure it'll be easy to convince her that we should limit WIP to be more efficient."

Tanya and Kay's Actual Conversation

Reminder: read the right-hand column first, then go back and read right to left.

What Tanya thought and felt	What Tanya and Kay said
Kay is really going to like this!	Tanya: I have a solution for you! We can finally stop pressuring you all the time to finish your testing before the sprint release.
Adding capacity at the bottleneck isn't scalable, and we don't have budget anyway. I'll just explain.	Kay: Great! Are we hiring another tester? We clearly need one.
Kay will be able to see the benefit, I'm sure. I just can't tell where we should set the WIP limit to start.	Tanya: Well, it's actually better than hiring. What we'll do is limit the number of tickets that go into the "Ready for QA" column. Would three be about right?
Hmm, she needs more explanation.	Kay: Hang on. Isn't that just going to annoy the engineers more? They'll have changes piling up earlier in the process.
We saw a great diagram in the course that should make it clear.	Tanya: No, that's the beauty of it. They'll do fewer tickets to start with because of this thing called "pull." Let me show you.

I'm so disappointed! She's got the wrong end of the stick. Why won't she let me explain how much easier her job would be with a WIP limit?	*Kay: I'm very skeptical. The execs keep saying we need to get more done, not less. Maybe you can show me later—I have a test to finish for tomorrow's release.*
I don't get it—what went wrong here?	*Tanya: Okay, maybe after tomorrow's standup?*

For this first example, we'll provide *our* scores and a revised conversation, but try not to look at our results until you've tried the process yourself. And don't worry if you get very different scores or a wildly varying revised conversation. There are no *right* answers here; only *improvements* that work for you. (Review how to find the Question Fraction, unexpressed thoughts and feelings, and triggers, twitches, and tells on pages 39–43.)

The Question Fraction. There's one question mark in Tanya's right-hand column: "Would three be about right?" So we'll add 1 to the bottom of our question fraction. Is this a genuine question? Only Tanya knows for sure, but we suspect it isn't. She does want to know where the limit should be (she says so in the left-hand column), but it's hard to believe she'd accept a surprising answer—imagine what would happen if Kay said zero, one hundred, or "Five, but only if they're written in German." And when Kay does give a surprising response, Tanya certainly doesn't seem interested in changing her beliefs or behavior, instead continuing to explain her ideas more clearly and forcefully. So we decide that she had zero genuine questions, giving us a finished score of $\frac{0}{1}$.

Unexpressed thoughts and feelings. As far as we can see, almost nothing makes it across to the right-hand column, so almost everything in the left-hand column is underlined. Tanya thinks Kay will like the solution, that hiring won't work, and that Kay just needs a sufficiently clear explanation of WIP limits. At the end of the conversation, Tanya feels disappointed and confused, but she shares none of this with Kay.

Triggers, tells, and twitches. Without more examples, it's hard to firmly identify signals Tanya could use. But one possible tell is her repeated assertions in the left-hand column that Kay just needs more explanation, which we will circle and label as a possible tell. When she notices herself thinking this way, she may want to substitute another behavior.

Tanya and Kay's Revised Conversation

Here's a revised version of the conversation. Try scoring it and then decide whether you think it's more effective. Or would you approach Tanya's situation differently?

What Tanya thought and felt	What Tanya and Kay said
Let's see whether Kay is interested in hearing about WIP limits. I think they'd really help her.	Tanya: I just came back from the Lean Startup course and I have a new idea I think you'll like. Can I describe it and see what you think?
Great!	Kay: Sure. But I do have a test to finish.
Let's start slowly. Does she see the problem as I do?	Tanya: Yes, about that—it actually seems like engineers are always waiting for your tests at the end of the sprint. Do you agree that's inefficient, or do you see it differently?
Well, fifty-fifty here. She's proposing hiring, but we don't have the budget.	Kay: Of course. That's why I keep saying we need another tester.
I'd like to explain this, but I'm trying to learn not to jump to an explanation. Let's check first—is she open to another solution?	Tanya: I understand, but I think there might be a different solution besides hiring. I could explain the new idea—would that be interesting?
Whoa! I didn't realize what an emotional issue this is for Kay.	Kay: Frankly, no. I don't think any crazy new plan is going to help with the stack of tests I get dumped on me every sprint at the last minute.
Kay's emotions are more important than WIP limits. I'd like to talk about those first, if she's willing.	Tanya: It sounds like you're feeling unhappy with your workload and how you get assigned tests to do. That worries me more than the workload itself right now. Would you like to talk about that instead?

Conclusion: Over to You

Now try analyzing your own difficult conversations using the Four Rs technique you've learned in this chapter: Record, Reflect, Revise, and Role Play. These techniques will help you have some distance from the conversation so you can see it as another might.

To help the learning go faster, consider reviewing your conversations with other people—they will definitely see it as others do! If you are feeling very brave, consider sharing your analysis with the other person in the conversation to discover their point of view, and ask their advice on how you might have revised the conversation to communicate with them more effectively.

As you analyze your conversations, keep in mind that you already know the result you are after: you want to have the kind of productive conversations you espouse. As we demonstrated at the start of the chapter, Chris Argyris found that we almost universally know the behaviors that will generate the best decisions—behaviors that show we are transparent in sharing our information and reasoning and we are curious about the information and reasoning of others.[22] When we can operate with this theory of action, we can harness the strength of our diversity. However, when faced with the challenge of productive conflict, we instinctively shy away from the opportunity and instead adopt a defensive reasoning mind-set to try to minimize threats and embarrassment.

While this defensive reaction is understandable, it isn't acceptable for those of us who want the benefits of successful transformation. Transformation requires fundamental shifts in how we behave as an organization. Unless we are content to join the 84% of companies who attempt digital transformation and fail, we need to learn to harness our communication superpowers by first undertaking a *conversational* transformation.

Part II

Chapter 3

The Trust Conversation

Building trust is the most fundamental step in helping your team escape the Taylorist feature factory and build a high-performing culture. An executive who believes employees are not acting in good faith will not be able to accept commitments or provide support to meet them. A tech lead who conceals information from her team will never overcome fear. And a developer or product manager who suspects colleagues of harboring ulterior motives will be unable to propose or agree on an effective Why.

Because it is an absolute prerequisite for success in the other conversations, we start our "instruction manual" by investigating the elements of trust, analyzing trust-destroying and trust-building conversations, and constructing an effective recipe for the Trust Conversation.

By the end of this chapter, you will be able to:

- recognize low-trust relationships by finding misaligned stories,
- communicate vulnerability and predictability to be transparent and prepare the way for trust building, and
- unlock your curiosity by using "TDD for People" to discover differences in reasoning and to align your story with that of others.

Trust Comes First

Let's start our examination of trust by hunting it down in hidden, nonobvious places. We'll meet some of the key employees at a troubled but imaginary tech startup. Their woes are varied, but none of them have any idea that a hidden problem—a lack of trust—underlies all their difficulties.

The two founders battle every Friday over the Gantt chart.

"We can start the Facebook integration in six weeks."

"No, we need to move it to early March. We have to do the video upload first."

"But what about the new authentication system?"

None of these weeks-away events ever happen as planned, of course—someone is ill, or a critical bug pops up, or a feature has to be rebuilt. But still they fight over the future as if they can control it. Recently, they've been wondering whether a better roadmapping tool or some estimation training would help them get more accurate predictions.

The tech lead is at the end of his rope. After years in the trenches at multiple companies, he knows exactly what the team needs to deliver on time: good specs, accurate estimates, another QA. He explains this carefully and clearly, over and over, but doesn't seem to make any headway. He gets sullen, partial compliance from the developers, no recruitment budget from finance, and outright opposition from the product manager. No one seems to understand that he's in charge of delivery and the others need to fall in line with his plan. He's working on a responsibility matrix to show everyone what their roles are, which he thinks will finally get everyone marching in the same direction.

The product manager is trying to get the bug rate down. Developers never seem to understand how the whole system fits together. Each sprint, she gives them more and more detailed specifications to work from. The defect backlog keeps growing nevertheless, so recently she's been writing test plans to go with the specs too, with no visible effect. Last night, working late on yet another intricate feature description, she fell asleep at her desk and dreamed about a giant bug monster eating her product. On the train home, she decided that tomorrow she'll draw a big mind map on the whiteboard, showing the interconnections of the system components, so everyone can see what impact each change might have and where to test.

The problems these team members have are common. You've probably encountered one or more of them if you've spent any time at all on a software team. And their intended solutions are just the sort that Agile coaches, Scrum conferences, and software vendors recommend: another process, a different tool, more information flow. There are books and courses that will tell each of them, in step-by-step detail, exactly how to implement their plans. They can cite the Agile Manifesto and the Scrum Principles to give weight to their proposals. In fact, there's nothing wrong with any of these solutions except for one thing: every single one is guaranteed to fail.

Let us say that again in another way—there is *nothing* that our protagonists can do on their own to get better delivery or fewer bugs. Certifications look nice on the wall, a shorter sprint will result in more frequent releases, and a longer retrospective will produce more actions, but none of these changes will make a dent in the outcomes that matter.

To see what's really going on, let's examine the inner monologue of each participant—that is, *what stories they are telling themselves*:*

- **Founders**: "We can't possibly understand the technical issues, but there must be some way to go faster."
- **Tech lead**: "I know what to do, and I just need everyone else to follow me in implementing the obvious path forward."
- **Product manager (PM)**: "Developers are unable to comprehend the whole product; I have to give them the data they need to do their jobs."
- **Developers** (remember them?): "Nobody tells us anything because no one cares about us. We should just put our heads down and keep coding."

Armed with this (imaginary) telepathy, we can start to see why the intended unilateral changes are not going to work. The founders, believing they can't understand the technology, will put rubbish assumptions into their shiny new road-map software and get garbage predictions out. The product manager doesn't see role definition as a problem—her role in explaining features is perfectly clear—so she won't engage with the tech lead's responsibility matrix. And the developers are convinced they are being left out entirely, so the PM's mind map will be yet another wall decoration to ignore.

---

* Of course, we're using the fact that our characters are fictional to share with you their inner thoughts. In reality, you'll need to do a lot more work to discover what others' stories are—which is what most of the rest of the chapter is about!

The underlying problem is that the inner stories of the team members in this conversation do not align. Each story explains the situation in a coherent way, offers predictions about others' behavior, and helps the storyteller develop solutions—but none of the stories agree with each other. It's as if Ptolemy, Newton, and Einstein all got together to build a spaceship to Mars! No amount of process innovation or clever tooling is going to get that rocket to the right destination.

We have a name for aligned stories: Trust. If I say I trust you, I mean that I have expectations about what you will do that have been met before and that I believe will be met again. When I trust you, I can use the story we agree on to predict your behavior and evaluate my possible actions, so that we can cooperate effectively. We are likely to come up with jointly designed plans that we can execute in tandem, and we can explain our common story to others so they can align with us too.

Our definition of Trust is stronger than the typical one; if you look up the word in a dictionary, you'll find something about believing that the other party is truthful, reliable, or capable. Such a belief is certainly helpful for building a solid, trusting relationship among team members, but it isn't enough. I can have faith that you are genuine and dependable, and yet still have beliefs about your actions and motives that prevent our stories from aligning and poison our ability to cooperate.

By contrast, if our stories are fully aligned, you will never need to worry about me misunderstanding or undermining your efforts. With aligned stories, the founders will be able to involve developers in their prioritization discussions to keep goals realistic and achievable; the tech lead will discover that he doesn't have all the answers and that team members can work with him to improve the structure and process more effectively; and the product manager will find that she can replace detailed specs with conversations with motivated developers.

In the rest of this chapter, we'll explain exactly how to work with your team to align your stories through the Trust Conversation, starting with helping you to be vulnerable and predictable, and then showing you how to use Chris Argyris's Ladder of Inference.

As Enterprise Agile/DevOps Lead, Coach, and Manager Brad Appleton says, "The first thing to build is trust!"[1]

Nell's Trust Story

I'm Nell, the CTO of a small, online retail business. The CEO, Ian, doesn't seem to trust me; he's always overruling me on one decision or another. Our latest interaction really got me steamed, so I decided to analyze the conversation. I started with the first R: Record.

Nell and Ian's Conversation

Reminder: read the right-hand column first, then go back and read right to left.

What Nell thought and felt	What Nell and Ian said
Not this again. Why can't you leave us alone?	Ian: I've had it with our payment provider. We have to replace them.
They're the best in the business. Any alternative will be much worse.	Nell: Why would we do that? We've only been using them for three months. There were some teething problems, but everything's running smoothly now.
The income would be categorized right if they'd put in the correct data like we've trained them to do. Garbage in, garbage out.	Ian: Smoothly? No way. They've messed up our invoices every single month. Finance is having to manually reconcile. Again.
We aren't going to annoy our customers and my entire team just because the accountants can't read basic instructions.	Nell: Argh. I've told you before, they haven't set up the reporting correctly. The payments integration has been very reliable, and customer complaints are way down. If we just get the right product metadata—
Pulling rank, again! Why employ me when you're going to decide everything yourself?	Ian: Totally unacceptable. Finance is the lifeblood of this company, and if they're not happy, we have to replace the vendor. That's final.

Another payments integration three months after the first one. How am I going to explain this to the team?	*Nell: Okay, if you insist.*

Trust with Ian is at rock bottom. He seems to think I'm incompetent, and I definitely believe he's micromanaging and playing politics by knuckling under to Finance. I feel trapped in the situation, unable to escape his controlling behavior. I'd like to build trust to escape this painful experience, but I'm not sure where to start.

PREPARING: BE VULNERABLE

Aligning stories in the Trust Conversation is going to require something very difficult from you: sharing your current story. This means opening up your feelings and thoughts to someone else. By doing so, you risk getting hurt—a prominent example of the difficult emotional work we told you to expect back in the Introduction.

It will help you in the Trust Conversation if you've established yourself as being willing to be vulnerable beforehand—you will be more used to it yourself, and others will see you as approachable—as someone who is inviting others to share their stories as well.

To get past your natural instinct to protect your story, try getting yourself to blurt out "unsafe" things; for example, ask "dumb"-sounding questions or share your doubts about how you drew a particular conclusion. When you are transparent about what you know and what you don't know, you are being vulnerable, because you may not appear as rational and as knowledgeable as you might like. By contrast, trying to feel safe and avoid vulnerability—say, by pretending to be aware of something you haven't heard of—usually gives false information that moves your stories further apart; and if you are found out, it signifies to your conversation partner that you are not being honest about yourself. It verifies that your stories are indeed misaligned and degrades their trust in you.

In *Rising Strong: How the Ability to Reset Transforms the Way We Live, Love, Parent, and Lead*, Brené Brown uses the phrase, "The story I'm telling myself is . . ." when sharing internal reasoning.[2] For example:

"The story I'm telling myself is that no one here cares about doing the washing up, so the office kitchen is always smelly."

"The story I'm telling myself is that our users are cheapskates who demand the least expensive option."

"The story I'm telling myself is that you aren't working on this project because it's boring."

This phrase helps you to stay in a "learning mind-set," because it means being explicit with both yourself and others that your reasoning is based on limited evidence and that you are perhaps reasoning incorrectly. This is a useful antidote to the instinctual view that "what you see is all there is," described by Daniel Kahneman in *Thinking, Fast and Slow*;[3] it reminds you that there's a lot that you don't see. It also helps build empathy in the listener because he or she can understand where your story came from without being threatened by the narrative.

These unfamiliar techniques may seem awkward at first, but with practice, the idea of sharing your internal reasoning while also sharing that you aren't attached to it comes to feel natural. You'll see several examples of this type of behavior in the sample conversations near the end of this chapter.

PREPARING: BE PREDICTABLE

Vulnerability alone isn't enough. If you want to align your story with those of others, then you will also have to give them evidence that your story is actually predictive, that it matches your actions.

The opposite behavior is everywhere, usually in the form of unintended hypocrisy: the earnest dieter who discusses his latest weight-loss plan while having a burger with everything; the taxi driver who bemoans the awful drivers as she runs yellow lights and cuts off cars; the poster on the wall that proclaims "We respect our people" while bosses stand beneath it to berate their underlings.

Before you dismiss these as applying only to others, we recommend you think carefully about your own theories and actions—if you are human, we are sure you have several examples of story-behavior mismatch in your own life.

Preparing well for a Trust Conversation means overcoming, as much as you can, this natural human tendency, and aligning your own behavior and theory to demonstrate predictability. When you inevitably fail to do so, admit your error and ask others to help you align better in the future.

Aligning your actions to your own story is hard enough. But even when you're truly acting consistently with your beliefs, you may still have to do more to convince others that you are predictable.

Billy, a programmer one of us knew some years ago, had a firm theory about his bosses: they were out to get him, giving him impossible assignments and fantasy deadlines, and any new initiative had to be a sneaky trick by those nasty managers. He put this theory on show when his team gathered for its first Agile planning session, the intent of which was to sort through possible projects and select those that might make sense to pursue for the first sprint. As soon as a list of ten potential features went up on the board, even before the team had estimated any of the stories at the highest level, Billy announced in a loud voice that this meeting was the last straw and that he was going to quit. Puzzled, his manager took Billy aside and asked what was going on. "No one could do all ten of those projects in one sprint!" exclaimed Billy. "You're just trying to work us to death so you can replace us with outsourced drones."

Billy's negative story about management was so deeply engrained that he literally couldn't hear his manager explain, at the start of the planning session, that the team would be selecting only those stories that could comfortably fit into the sprint. There was more evidence, in the form of the planning session itself and in other Agile practices being introduced, that Billy could rely on his manager to look out for the team's needs, but he wasn't able to align this with the story he was telling himself yet.

Through a Trust Conversation with Billy, we learned that his theory had been firmly reinforced by employment in multiple abusive jobs, including one where senior leaders routinely erased team estimates from the kanban board and replaced them with their own ("I'm sure we can do this ten-point story by Friday," they'd say). It took many repeated experiences with managers who claimed to respect team needs, and then actually followed through with that respect, to build trust with Billy and create an alternate shared story.

We often find that you can establish initial predictability with small, highly visible steps that don't necessarily relate directly to the main issues of the Trust Conversation. For instance, in Billy's team of programmers, a constant irritant was repeated requests from nontechnical staff to fix the printer or the internet connection. His manager announced that this practice would end, and when no outsourced IT service could be found quickly enough, he proceeded to crawl around on the floor himself, chasing cables and resetting routers. This clearly showed Billy and his colleagues that when the manager made a promise, it would be kept, and it helped establish a clear reputation for predictability that was very useful in building trust in other areas.

The Conversation: TDD for People

Kent Beck says that Test-Driven Development (TDD), the practice of writing a test concurrently with the code it exercises, gives him "a sense of comfort and intimacy."[4] That is exactly the feeling we want you to have during the Trust Conversation, and the tool to help you achieve it is the Ladder of Inference, another concept from Chris Argyris and colleagues (see Figure 3.1).[5]

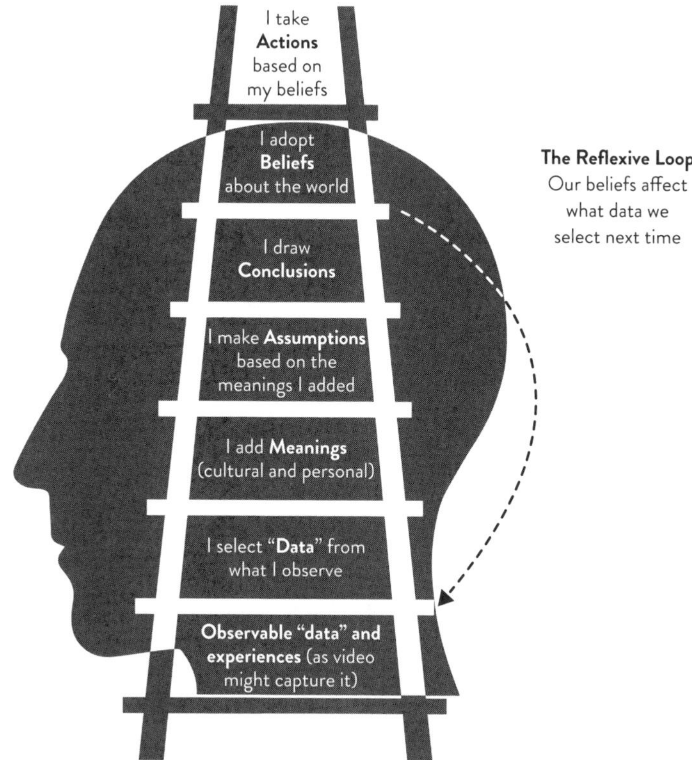

Adapted from Peter Senge, The Fifth Discipline.

Figure 3.1: The Ladder of Inference

Observe that the Ladder tells a coherent story: from data, you derive meanings, which gives you assumptions, conclusions, and beliefs; and from these, you determine your actions. The goal of the Trust Conversation is to align your story with that of your conversation partner, and the Ladder provides an obvious way to structure that alignment: first align on the bottom rung, then rung 2, and so on, until your stories match.

This would be easy if both parties' ladders were visible, but as you can see from Figure 3.1, only the bottom rung (observations) and the top rung (actions) exist outside your head, where others can see them. Everything else is invisible—which is where TDD for People comes in. As Argyris, Putnam, and McLain Smith say:

> It should be clear that the likelihood of differences in the interpretations of different observers increases the higher one goes on the ladder of inference. Hence some cardinal rules...are: Begin at the lowest rung of the ladder of inference, state the meanings at the next higher rung and check for agreement, and continue to the next higher rung only if there is agreement at [the] lower rungs. These rules are meant not only for action scientists but also for agents in everyday life, whenever they are dealing with important and threatening issues.[6]

When writing code with TDD, you proceed slowly, in confident, small steps. Similarly, when using the Ladder of Inference, you are going to ascend in small, tested steps, each of which increases your confidence. At each step, you'll ask a genuine question of your partner about her reasoning at that rung and if needed, explain your own reasoning as well. (We described *genuine questions* in more detail in Chapter 2.) This will reveal both sides' ladders rung by rung, so you can understand where they differ. When your test fails—that is, when you are surprised by or don't understand the answer to your question, exposing a misalignment—you'll stop, refactor your understanding, and retry the test. At the end, you and your partner will have more closely aligned your ladders and, therefore, your stories; and where you still don't fully agree, you will at least understand each other's motives. As a result, you will have built substantial trust for the future.

Let's go through an example: Suppose your team is working on a system that sets and adjusts prices for customers, and you have noticed one recently added team member, Helen, griping that the pricing algorithm is too complex to maintain. Since others, including you, are working on this code happily, you believe there is a misalignment that is affecting trust, as Helen's complaints sap morale and she resists all suggestions for improving the problem code. You are starting to suspect that she and perhaps others are going to refuse to update prices until the whole subsystem is rewritten, which you don't think the company can afford right now.

Rung 1: Observable Data. "Helen, I heard you say in the standup that the pricing code is overengineered. Did I understand you correctly?"

"Yes, anyone can see it's impenetrable."

You have established the basis for the conversation—that Helen sees a complexity problem. Your test is green; move to the next step.

Rung 2: Data Selection. "Got it. For me, the important part of any complex code is its architecture—how it's divided into chunks—because that's hardest to change. Is that the area of most concern for you too?"

"Absolutely. I mean, the comments and variable names suck, but we can refactor to improve those over time. I can't see how any new joiner can hope to understand a forest of tiny classes like we have, though."

After hearing your reasoning, Helen has confirmed agreement. Green again. (Notice we don't have to agree with Helen that the architecture is actually objectively complex—just that she perceives it that way.)

Rung 3: Meanings. "Okay. So that means to me that you are going to find it hard to add new prices to the system. Is that right?"

"Of course! That's why I asked to be reassigned to the edit page design."

Your stories continue to match; Helen agrees that the perceived complexity is a barrier to her work. Green test: onward!

Rung 4: Assumptions. "So are you assuming that the pricing algorithm is just too hard for you to work on?"

"Sure, but it's not just me—Ramona says she can't make heads or tails of it either."

A new fact: Helen isn't alone in her assessment of the code. But this is another green test—your stories continue to match. You may be starting to wonder where the misalignment is, or whether it exists.

Rung 5: Conclusions. "I guess you're thinking that we're ripe for a rewrite of that code then."

"What? No, that would be a waste of time. You and the other experts can keep hacking at it while us newbies stick to the user interface."

RED! Here's the misalignment. You thought Helen was angling for an expensive overhaul, but she's suggesting that only experienced team members work on the complex algorithm. Time to refactor!

Rung 5: Conclusions, again. "Ah, I didn't understand your thinking. You're concluding that the pricing complexity means new joiners like you can't work on that code, is that right?"

"Of course; that's what I keep saying. We just don't have enough experience to make changes safely."

Now we're green again; we understand Helen's thinking, even if we aren't aligned with the actions it leads to. On to the next rung but with new understanding.

Rung 6: Beliefs. "So it sounds like you believe that making some tasks off-limits to newer team members is a good idea. I have a different belief, though—that we should raise everyone's skills until they can work on any feature; so everyone learns and we get the most from every developer. What are your thoughts?"

"I did think that I had to stick to the easier bits. But I can get behind the training idea, if we can afford it."

Here's alignment happening in real time. Now that your conclusions match, it's easier for Helen to bring her beliefs in line with yours. Green!

Rung 7: Actions. "Great! I'd be willing to book Maria, our pricing expert, to spend the next week training you and Ramona on the pricing algorithm. Would that work?"

"Sure! I didn't know that was an option. I'd be willing to give it a try!"

We've reached an action that Helen agrees with, thanks to aligning our stories. Even better, Helen can apply the common story to other potentially challenging areas, asking for training or help to raise her skills rather than complaining about being unable to contribute. In other words, we have built trust with Helen.

Scoring TDD for People

To score a conversation with TDD for People in mind, label your statements and questions in either column with the rung they correspond to. If you start at the bottom of the Ladder, with Data, Selections, and Meanings, and then move up to Assumptions, Conclusions, and Beliefs as the conversation progresses, you're on track. But if you're spending most of your time at the top of the Ladder, consider ways to consciously bring yourself back down to the lower rungs before proceeding.

Let's return to Nell's conversation, found on pages 57–58, and see if she can use TDD for People to come up with a more honest conversation.

Nell's Trust Story Continued

Reflecting, Revising, and Role Playing

I started by doing the basic scoring for my conversation. I have one disingenuous question, which I asked only to get Ian to change his mind—a unilateral, Model I approach that didn't work. I shared only one or two items from the left-hand column. And my "Argh" halfway through was a pretty obvious tell, showing I was giving up in frustration.

Then I scored the conversation for TDD for People, which was even worse. I spent almost all my time in Conclusions or above, with only a couple of visits to Data or to Meanings just to bolster my argument. I definitely wasn't being very transparent or curious here.

Finally, I decided on some revised actions to take next time. I'm going to try forcing myself to ask about Data, Meanings, and Assumptions before going further up the Ladder. I'm also going to try sharing my reasoning more and noticing when I'm starting to get frustrated. I tried to Role Play with my friend, the sales director, who also clashes with Ian, which gave us both some practice in going slowly up the Ladder.

Improved Conversation

Ian proposed we adopt Blaze as our new payment provider. After I rejected it as being too difficult to work with, he scheduled a meeting with its team anyway. I'm angry that he doesn't trust me to make the decision and is overruling me yet again, but I also want to understand his reasoning by trying out the techniques I developed in my analysis.

Nell and Ian's Revised Conversation

What Nell thought and felt	What Nell and Ian said
Let's get the facts straight first—stay at the bottom of the Ladder.	Nell: I see that the Blaze team is coming in on Wednesday, is that right?
What a waste of time! Their references were terrible. Wait, I'm racing ahead and starting to get frustrated—I should stay focused on the next rung.	Ian: Yes, it is. I thought we should have a look at the system in person.
Okay, he did invite them. Let's find out what that means while sharing the meaning it has for me.	Nell: That means they're still in the running to become our new provider, right?
At least he read my report.	Ian: Well, not really. Their current users told you their support was useless, didn't they?
This doesn't make any sense. Is he up to something?	Nell: Yes, but now I'm really confused. Why did you book the visit if I'd eliminated them?
I never heard of using a vendor as a practice target before. Can you do that??	Ian: Well, I want to make sure we have a solid filtering process for the next few candidates, and I thought we could practice with Blaze.
Hmm, this isn't what I feared. The meaning he has is different from what I thought it would be.	Nell: I get it—kind of a dry run.
That would definitely be good for my team—some of them have never done any software selection before.	Ian: Exactly. The other vendors can't visit in person, and I thought it would be easier for our team to try out their questions with someone in the room before doing it over the phone.

How is Blaze going to feel about this?	Nell: That makes sense. Seems unfair to the vendor, though.
	Ian: Maybe, but the reps do have the chance to wow us during the visit and turn us around. I'll be surprised if they do, though.
Boy, do I feel better having clarified Ian's thinking. He wasn't overruling me after all!	Nell: Me too!

Wow, that shifted my thinking completely. I only got a short distance up the Ladder of Inference, to the Meanings rung, before the realization hit me. Now, instead of the story I started with—"Ian doesn't listen and just does what he wants"—I am starting to believe that "Ian listens to my opinions and wants my team to learn to select vendors well."

If we keep confirming this shared story, it will become much easier for me to trust him in the future and for us both to jointly design solutions to our partner-management problems.

Example Trust Conversations

Now let's dig a little deeper and look at some more examples of the Trust Conversation in action.

Ursula and the Development Team: Explaining Reasoning

Ursula says, "As the founder of our startup, I've tentatively decided to hire a new CTO, even though he had a disastrous on-site interview with most of the development team. I want to explain my thinking to the team—Al, Betsy, and Carlos—and answer what I expect will be tough questions from unhappy engineers."

Ursula and the Developers' Conversation

What Ursula thought and felt	What Ursula and the developers said
Best get it all out to start.	Ursula: I've decided to hire Zeb as our new CTO. I know that won't be popular, but I want to explain why I've made this decision.
Ouch. Al's no diplomat—but what if he's right about Zeb?	Al: You're nuts. He told us our main product was crap and has to be rebuilt.
Can't hide from the truth.	Ursula: I know Zeb's approach in the interviews was terrible. Are you willing to hear about how I made this decision despite that?
A skeptical crowd, as I expected.	Betsy: Okay, but this better be good.
Let's start with observable data. Am I missing anything here?	Ursula: Great. I see Zeb as extremely experienced and very opinionated. Do you see him that way or differently?
Glad Zeb's skills did come through.	Carlos: Sure, he knows his stuff all right.
We really need expertise—most of the team have never built anything like our product before.	Ursula: And to me, that means he has a lot to bring an inexperienced team like ours.
An excellent question.	Betsy: Yes, but how can he teach us anything when he's being a jerk all the time?
I'm certain I can get Zeb to soften his approach, but I wonder if the team shares my confidence.	Ursula: My assumption is that he can learn to build relationships and manage well, if I coach him personally. Do you think that's possible?
No surprise Al is opposed; he took the brunt of the criticism from Zeb.	Al: You're a great coach, Ursula, but Zeb is beyond hope, even for you.

Can we agree to disagree here?	Ursula: I respect your view, Al; but I've coached many difficult people, and I see huge potential for learning in Zeb. Are you willing to let me try?
Glad Al is willing to give me a chance.	Al: I'll be amazed if you pull it off, but okay.
How about the others?	Ursula: And of course you may turn out to be right, Al. How about the rest of you? Do you share my conclusion that Zeb is worth a shot, if I give him frequent, personal guidance? I'll lengthen his probation period to three months to allow us all to see how he performs.
There we go.	Carlos: Sure. Betsy: I'm willing to try.
Ready to move ahead now that we have shared reasoning.	Ursula: Great, thank you. My belief is that we can find out in short order whether Zeb is right for us. I'll check back every few weeks on how you're feeling, okay?

Ursula could easily have just imposed her will on the team, unilaterally announcing Zeb's start date. Instead, she shared her reasoning and partially aligned her story with the team's. Not everyone agrees, especially Al, whose expectations remain very different from Ursula's. But the differences are now discussable, and the team knows that Ursula will be accountable to them for Zeb's coaching progress.

Isaac and Erin: Surprised by Feedback

Isaac says, "Erin runs operations, and I'm a developer. We often build features that are supposed to make life easier for her team, so we talk often. She asked for feedback as part of a 'personal retrospective' for self-improvement, and I gave it to her—but the conversation didn't go the way I expected."

Issac and Erin's Conversation

What Isaac thought and felt	What Isaac and Erin said
I'd like to help. She needs to know how hard it is to approach her.	Erin: Thanks for helping me with feedback, Isaac. Where should I look to improve?
I'll soften the blow—in fact, most of us don't even try asking for more detail any more.	Isaac: Well, you could help your team file clearer bugs and feature requests. And as you probably know, some of us avoid asking you for clarification because you can be a bit intimidating.
Whoa! Why such a strong reaction? She did ask for the feedback, so what did she expect?	Erin: Intimidating?! Where does that come from?
She's living up to her reputation, all right. I'll stay at the bottom of the ladder to start.	Isaac: I notice that you're looking red in the face and speaking louder. Is that—
At least I'm not alone in seeing this pattern.	Erin: Of course I am! I keep hearing that I'm "scary," but I bend over backward to stay accessible and get feedback.
Okay, instead of guessing, I'll find out explicitly what her reaction means.	Isaac: It sounds like hearing this really concerns you. Is that right? How are you feeling?
How can she not see how she's scaring others off?	Erin: Annoyed and depressed—I can't shake this undeserved reputation. It's the opposite of what I want and what I observe. Is there a single real example of me frightening someone?
This conversation is a great example!	Isaac: Well, I'm feeling a little intimidated right now by your reaction.
Hmm, I actually can't come up with another example. What does that mean?	Erin: That's fair, and I'm sorry. The feedback is really hard to hear. But this doesn't happen when someone asks me to clarify a bug report.

I hadn't thought about it, but we actually never ask Erin directly. It's always Maria who tells us to buzz off.	*Isaac: Actually, you're right. Come to think of it, it's normally Maria in your team who has the most dismissive reactions.*
A fair question.	*Erin: So why do you see me as the intimidating one?*
She does put the responsibility on Erin.	*Isaac: I guess because she says you are telling her not to spend time helping us.*
That was surprisingly helpful.	*Erin: I think we may have found the problem—I haven't been clear in my direction to Maria and the rest of my team. Thanks for thinking this through with me.*

The Trust Conversation isn't always something you can plan for; here, it snuck up on Isaac when he didn't expect it. It would have been easy to react to Erin's outburst in kind, with something like, "There you go again, blasting someone who's only trying to help you," but that would have been skipping all the way to the top of the Ladder of Inference and would not have built trust. Instead, Isaac managed to stay on the bottom rungs (Data, Selections, and Meanings), and after reflection, discovered his own perceptions and feedback weren't as accurate as he'd thought. Erin and Isaac now have shared stories about bug reports and Erin's wish to be responsive, which should help them work together with greater trust.

CASE STUDY: TRUST SAVES THE DAY

Walled Off

"I just want the developers to be happy," said Paul Joyce, founder of Geckoboard, a maker of dashboard software. "Productivity and profit can come later. Right now, I'd just like to see them enjoying their jobs." I (Squirrel) nodded and wondered what was making the engineers so depressed.

It was certainly obvious to me, after only a day on site, that something wasn't right in Geckoboard's small tech team of ten. In the spacious tech room, cluttered with board games and Ruby books, there were four standups every day but little to report in each. Retrospectives were stilted and unproductive. Meetings dragged on for hours with little energy or output. Conflicts over technology or process were expressed indirectly, if at all. There were plenty of projects underway—nearly as many as there were developers to carry them out!—but none showed signs of being finished anytime soon. Ironically, one of the company's own dashboards hung on the wall of the tech room, displaying a huge graph that showed revenue remaining stubbornly flat, missing every monthly target so far that year.

Unsurprisingly, a similar malaise afflicted the rest of the business, whose desks were crowded into the other room of the small London office. Customer Service team members tried to talk positively about the product but couldn't tell users when to expect bug fixes. Marketing and Sales wanted to splash new features to attract interest but had nothing to shout about. Paul himself was feeling disappointed and isolated, seeing no way to get the organization out of first gear. In fact, the only cheery presence in view was Mr. White, the office dog, who barked to announce arrivals, and chased toys up and down the hallway.

As I watched Mr. White run back and forth, I noticed something odd: he was going through the doorway between the two rooms, *but no one else was*. These two groups were separated by a wall, not only physical but psychological. They barely said hello to each other when they arrived for the day and said precious little else as the day went on. Unlike Mr. White, they stayed in their respective rooms and rarely ventured into each other's territory. What had happened to divide these two groups, I wondered? Why couldn't they cooperate?

Delivering and Engaging

The first step, I decided, was to show predictable progress. We consolidated the standups and shut down all projects but one, an integration with a popular product that seemed likely to get customers excited and paying more. Delivering incrementally on this single result built energy and interest within the development team, and productivity and mood started to lift. A natural leader, Leo, emerged from the team, and began removing obstacles and increasing efficiency. Gradually and gingerly, trust began to grow among the developers and product managers. They had had to be vulnerable to make their initial commitment, but eventually the predictable delivery of small wins increased their confidence in each other.

Even so, Mr. White was still the only regular commuter between the two halves of the company. The engineers described to me their negative stories about the rest of the business: "No one cares about fixing bugs," "They don't tell us what sales are coming next," "Paul doesn't care about employees." And Paul told me about feeling isolated, disempowered, and uninvolved, even as the developers were starting to deliver more. There was clearly more to do.

To start, we created opportunities for interaction—holding show-and-tell sessions for Sales, inviting support staff to retrospectives. Crucially, we brought Paul into standups, where he was able to show some vulnerability by sharing his sense of isolation and his frustrations with the unmoving financial metrics. I also led a brief session for everyone on TDD for People, with the expectation that this tool would help the two sides share stories and increase trust.

The Trust Conversation

The crucial breakthrough came when Leo and Paul sat down for what turned out to be a Trust Conversation. Leo and I had role played it to prepare, and he knew he wanted to start by asking about the biggest obstacle to trust for him: the recent and seemingly sudden departure of two key employees. By asking questions like "When did you decide they had to go?" "What did they do wrong?" and "What did their exit mean to you?" Leo was able to share his story—that Paul had dismissed the two quickly and thoughtlessly—and understand Paul's, which involved making agonizing decisions after sleepless nights, and much more negotiation and discussion behind closed doors than Leo had thought.

By the end of the conversation, Leo was starting to believe that Paul's actions were much more compassionate and considerate than he had thought before; and Paul could see at last why some in the tech team, thinking he was "trigger happy" and ready to fire on a whim, had retreated from him, rebuffing his attempts to inspire and lead.

Trust Breaks Down the Wall

It's not an understatement to say that the Trust Conversation between Leo and Paul was the turning point in improving relationships and performance across the whole organization. With Leo's support, Paul was able to engage much more closely with the developers, and then to bring others from the "nontech" room into demos and design sessions for successful interactions.

And engineers, singly and in groups, were able to question Paul about previous decisions, building faith that he and others in the rest of the business were not acting capriciously. Over time, the greater cooperation between the two "sides" led to better product decisions and improved customer satisfaction.

Today, four years later, Leo is now the VP of Engineering and works closely with Paul in a mutually trusting relationship. Employees use the Ladder of Inference regularly, and collaboration between developers and nontechnical people is common; some support staff even learned to code and formed their own development team. Customer engagement is up, and revenue is moving in the right direction.

Oh, and Geckoboard moved to a new office last year—with no wall down the middle.

Conclusion: Applying the Trust Conversation

In this chapter, you learned about the importance of internal stories, how to show others that you are willing and able to change your story through vulnerability and predictability, and the "TDD for People" technique for aligning your story with that of someone else to build trust. Aligned stories allow us to safely adopt the transparency and curiosity that we need for a successful conversational transformation. You can use the Trust Conversation in many ways, including the following:

- An ***executive leader*** can create a trusting relationship with employees, giving confidence to all parties that the cultural transformation is headed in the right direction without micromanagement and continual supervision.
- A ***team lead*** can align stories with her team to eliminate unproductive infighting and debates, and instead, cooperate to meet sprint goals and product targets.
- An ***individual contributor*** can boost trust with his peers for more effective collaboration, so he can get and give more help with cooperative activities like code reviews, estimations, and pairing sessions.

Chapter 4

The Fear Conversation

Neither of us have ever seen a fearful Agile (or Lean or DevOps) team that has also been successful. Fear is one of the biggest inhibitors of transformation. An organization may suffer from fear of error, of failure, of building the wrong product, of disappointing managers, of exposing poor leadership, of any number of other disasters. Whatever its particular subject, fear paralyzes the team, inhibiting creativity and cooperation. A compliant, fearful team fits well into a Taylorist factory, where no thinking is required; but to function outside the factory in a collaborative, high-performing culture, you need not only the Trust you built in the last chapter but also the *psychological safety* you will construct in this one.

We therefore continue our how-to guide with methods that will help you uncover your own fears, locate and understand the fears of others, and lead a Fear Conversation to mitigate fear on all sides. You will find these techniques beneficial whether you are a CTO whose organization resists every attempt to organize cross-functionally, a system architect yearning to help her team develop the courage to try a new messaging pattern, or a designer afraid of proposing a potentially unpopular user journey. In this chapter, you will learn to be *transparent* about your and your team's fears and *curious* about how to mitigate them.

When you finish mastering these techniques, you will be able to:

- Identify practices and habits in your team that are unsafe but have become accepted as "how we do it here." This *normalization of deviance* is a signal that there is a hidden fear to be uncovered and addressed.
- Overcome your natural, effortless tendency to jump to conclusions by using *Coherence Busting*. The coherent stories that your brain accepts without question are almost certainly blinding you to alternative ways to see events, including legitimate fears affecting some or all of your team.
- Jointly create a *Fear Chart* to uncover team fears by using the previous two techniques to generate candidate fears to consider, and then, most important, mitigate these fears effectively.

Fear: The Default Feeling

Imagine two of our preagricultural ancestors, Og and Ug, whose tribe subsists on whatever they can pluck from the bushes or bludgeon to death with stones. The two go out together one day to hunt rabbits, but as soon as they enter a clearing in the woods, the hunters freeze. The tall grass is parting as something much larger than a rabbit passes through it, and both can hear the faint but growing sound of huge feet on dirt.

Og thinks, *I wonder what that large animal is? Could be a deer—food for the whole tribe!* Full of curiosity, Og strides boldly forward to meet the unknown beast, rock held high.

Ug thinks, *Oh no, it's a large animal—probably a hungry bear! We should get out of its way!* Terrified and panicked, Ug shimmies up the nearest tree.

You can finish the story yourself, of course. The point is that *all of us are descended from Ug*. If you default to curiosity when confronted with new and unknown data, odds are you will not make it to a ripe old age in the forest. If, instead, you default to fear, you will likely live to have many children and to pass on your instinctual fear to them.

The problem with the Legacy of Ug is that it is very poorly suited to modern society, where deer (opportunities for learning) far outnumber bears (catastrophic outcomes of experiment). Your team, encountering customer opposition to a new version or an unexpected demand from Marketing, is very likely to react like good Ug-descended tree climbers—delaying the release or rejecting the new feature request. We don't have many courageous Ogs around, who would instinctively find a way to get the software out or insert the story into the sprint. And so we lose opportunities to learn right and left, and we wonder why our teams don't iterate and improve the way we think they are supposed to.

In Amy Emondson's *Teaming: How Organizations Learn, Innovate, and Compete in the Knowledge Economy*, Edmondson calls the Og state "psychological safety."[1] A team with this characteristic has a "climate of openness," readily and fearlessly discussing problems and trying experiments to address them. For instance, she found that although you might think nursing groups who report few operational errors are the best performers, exactly the opposite is true; those who report more mistakes get more opportunities to learn and therefore get better results.[2] Kent Beck, in *Extreme Programming Explained: Embrace Change*, also exhorts Agile teams to "value courage," with practices like constant refactoring and frequent feedback.[3] And as you may recall from Chapter 1, Allspaw and Hammond urge DevOps practitioners to fearlessly accept that "failure will happen."[4]

The Fear Conversation will help you create psychological safety and courage in your team by revealing fears and making it okay to mitigate them. The difficult emotional work is in sharing your fears and those of your conversation partner—requiring honesty and vulnerability—and uncovering information that allows you both to mitigate the risks that are frightening each of you.*

A team we worked with labored under the weight of years of code neglect—impenetrable modules that performed some vital, unknown function; features that were so tightly coupled that manual testing was impossible, never mind running the (nonexistent) unit tests; buttons labeled "don't press this button." One developer innocently opened a webpage to see what it was for and it ran an invisible script that reduced many prices on the site by a thousandfold!

Understandably, this environment released the team's inner Ugs, and the whole group was paralyzed with the fear that any change, however small, might unleash a catastrophe. Afraid of being embarrassed by causing a bug, they refused to commit and release their code, creating larger and larger batches of work rather than small, frequent deliveries. Repeated exhortations to "ask for forgiveness, not permission" fell on deaf ears, and progress was glacial at best.

The Fear Conversation revealed that developers believed they would be reprimanded or fired if their actions turned out badly, and there were valid

---

* Naturally, a prerequisite for a successful Fear Conversation is trust—if you don't have this, your team won't be willing to discuss fears. See the previous chapter if your team lacks the aligned stories that constitute trust.

reasons to believe this, as executives had previously punished individuals or the whole team for failure. Yet it also turned out that the organization was, in fact, very risk friendly: wrong results or even downtime had few consequences, and certainly none that would outweigh the cost of delaying improvements.*

Once all parties had revealed their fears through the Fear Conversation, we could begin being creative in developing risk mitigations. We moved the developers' seats close to the Customer Service team, who was always the first to hear about site problems, and agreed that programmers would keep their ears open for issues from the next bank of desks. And we provided a big red button that, when pressed, would revert the most recent release instantly. Finally, we wrote "YES" in giant letters on a whiteboard, and silently pointed to it when anyone asked whether we should release. As a result, it became common to hear "Site down!" from the call center, followed seconds later by "It's back up!" from the engineering side, as they gleefully punched the big red reset button.

Releases started to happen daily, then multiple times a day; and internal and external customers were delighted with the rapid progress we had unlocked. Creating psychological safety through the Fear Conversation had allowed the team to dramatically improve their results across the board.

Next, we'll look at how to prepare for the Fear Conversation by seeking out the "normalization of deviance" and creating a frame to guide the conversation.

Tara's Fear Story

I'm Tara, one of two founders of a small startup that provides a feedback-tracking product to sales teams. Every week I dread my planning meeting with my cofounder, Matt, who looks after our technology team. I'm fearful that we're going to let down our customers, and I'm angry that we aren't building the complete, functional product that they expect. The planning meeting only confirms these fears, as Matt makes excuse after excuse for not building what our clients need.

* The thousandfold price reduction, once corrected, actually delighted the marketing department, who promptly issued a humorous press release about the amazing deals enabled by the engineering error and crowed about the boost in traffic that resulted.

During the last planning session, I felt so upset that I got physically ill. I hope that analyzing the conversation will help me find a way out of this situation, starting with the recording of what we said below.

Tara and Matt's Conversation

Reminder: read the right-hand column first, then go back and read right to left.

What Tara thought and felt	What Tara and Matt said
What a catastrophe!	Matt: We can't get to sorting or filtering in the new report this sprint.
We have to get these features in—users are demanding them.	Tara: What?! Don't you want people to use it? The user research told us very clearly that users expect to be able to sort, at least.
This is just a way of saying that you don't care enough to get it done.	Matt: Of course I do. But what we can deliver is limited by time and skill. A static report is what we've estimated as deliverable by Friday.
What's really happening is that you aren't pushing hard enough.	Tara: Why? Can't the team work harder? Are they not motivated enough?
This is nonsense. The engineers are lazy, and you're enabling them.	Matt: That's not the problem, Tara. Working harder would, in fact, be counterproductive—they'd make silly mistakes and go slower. We just have to accept the estimates.
If our developers can't get off their butts, maybe someone from the outside will be able to show them how it's done.	Tara: Okay, so maybe we should hire a contractor. Would that get the report done?
You shoot down everything I propose. You've obviously just made up your mind that this isn't happening.	Matt: No. Remember the last contractor? She took weeks to get up to speed. A new joiner would slow us down this sprint, not speed us up.

I had two blog posts and a webinar lined up to promote this feature. I'll have to delay them all, just when we desperately need a new sales angle. I'm completely deflated.

Tara: I guess there's no way out. We'll just have to wait before starting to promote the new report.

I felt so ill after this conversation—nauseated, chest pounding—that I thought I must be having a heart attack. Why does Matt keep ignoring clear feedback from our customers and refusing to ask the engineers to do more? I thought he cared about this business as much as I do, but I am really beginning to doubt that. If we don't find a way to get these features completed, we're going to miss our targets and go bankrupt, which terrifies me.

PREPARING: NORMALIZATION OF DEVIANCE

The goal of the Fear Conversation is to discover hidden fears and make them discussable. But how do they get hidden in the first place?

Part of the answer lies in a nondescript waiting room at Columbia University, where researchers Bibb Latané and John Darley told a group of students to fill in a questionnaire as part of a psychology experiment. After a few minutes, smoke began to flow into the room from a wall vent. Everyone kept writing; none of the students said a word. More smoke billowed in, and it became hard to see. Nothing happened. No one made a move to get help or even asked what was going on. Eventually, the acrid smoke led to coughing and watering eyes, and one participant opened a window—but the dogged students continued writing, not discussing the unfolding crisis or seeking assistance until the experimenters stepped in and terminated the exercise.[5]

The phenomenon on display here is variously known as the *bystander effect* or, our favorite term, *pluralistic ignorance*. Individuals are uncomfortable with an event or observation, but since others are not acting, they (wrongly) assume that everyone else thinks the situation is normal and safe, and don't act themselves.*

* The influence of the group is clearly shown by a variation of the smoke experiment that Latané and Darley tried: if you ask a student to wait *alone* in the same room with the same smoke coming through the vent, she will act quickly to get help.

A common fear is felt by some or all of the people involved, but the expression of that fear is inhibited by the apparent consensus of the rest of the group. In other words, *people would rather die in a fire than be the first of the group to report the smoke*. That's how strong pluralistic ignorance is.

The smoke experiment tells us how people react to a singular frightening occurrence, but what happens if a fear-inducing event occurs over and over with no action in response? In *The* Challenger *Launch Decision: Risky Technology, Culture, and Deviance at NASA*, Diane Vaughan investigates the space shuttle explosion in 1986;[6] and Richard Feynman, in an appendix to the *Rogers Commission Report*, separately analyzed NASA's responses to problems observed during launches of the space shuttle on cold days.[7] Both observed what Vaughan called the *normalization of deviance*: Because the shuttle had launched without calamity over and over in cold conditions, NASA concluded that cracks observed in booster components on such flights were not a problem. Although no cracks at all in the O-rings were expected, the fact that they were small in size led some engineers to conclude the danger they posed was low. Others had concerns—What reason could there be for believing that the next crack would be as small as the previous ones?—but did not speak up loudly enough to stop the flights.

In fact, NASA managers believed so strongly in the safety of shuttle launches that they decided it was a good idea to put a civilian teacher on the *Challenger* flight of January 28, 1986. That morning, with icicles forming on the launch tower, the boosters exploded exactly as the engineers had feared they would, killing the entire crew.

The phenomenon of flickering tests, or tests that randomly fail, in software development teams illustrates how normalization of deviance can affect a team, though with much less dire consequences. Developers build an automated test suite and run it on every code change. They observe that a few of the tests succeed most of the time but fail at seemingly random moments. The natural conclusion is that the tests are erroneous—they "flicker" occasionally due to some testing anomaly—and can be rerun if they fail. If they succeed after a few tries, a release can go ahead. As many of us know too well, the result is a production failure when the flickering test turns out to be alerting us to a real but intermittent fault.

In both cases, that of the O-ring cracks and the flickering tests, we have an *espoused* norm for the group: "don't fly with broken equipment" and "don't release when tests fail." But repeated experience with a deviation from this norm—"flying safely with cracked rings" and "releasing despite intermittent failure"—leads to a new *norm-in-use*, with the organization ignoring its own alarm systems. Thanks to pluralistic ignorance, expression of fear about the dangers of the new norm are repressed, and everything is in place for a disastrous outcome.

Symptom	Espoused Norm	Norm-In-Use
Obvious bugs in production	Pass tests consistently	Tests can fail sometimes
System alerts hourly	Clear alerts promptly	Ignore known harmless alerts
Sprint end date extended	End sprint cleanly and on time	Lengthen sprint to cram in more
Long standups	Keep standups crisp and speedy	Give lengthy status reports
Low code quality	Refactor frequently	Take shortcuts often
Too many bugs	Full test coverage	Tests are optional
Minimal iteration	Release frequently	Release only when certain
Too many admins	Grant permissions only where needed	Grant admin rights on request
Improvement actions not done	Use retrospectives effectively	Too busy to do the actions
Users confused and frustrated	Involve customers/users in the design	Skip user research

Table 4.1: Examples of Normalized Deviance

The Fear Conversation helps uncover the hidden fears in our team and replaces normalization of deviance with the psychological safety needed to notice and correct errors swiftly. To prepare for it, look for examples of a dangerous, deviant norm in your organization. To get you started, see our examples in Table 4.1, where we list a number of symptoms you might observe and, for each symptom, an espoused norm that is being violated and a norm-in-use that is actually being followed.

As you can see from the table, deviances of this kind may appear anywhere—in your software, your Agile processes, your product design, your executive team. They may seem easy to spot, but in practice, they're not so apparent; by definition, normalized deviance means the whole team, including you, has likely become blind to the variation from the espoused norm.

Have a colleague or friend from outside the team look for deviations with you, as their outside perspective can help you identify problems you can't see from within. If your team experiences outages, severe bugs, or other serious failures, analyze these events with your colleague and seek examples of violated norms. Reflect on what deviations might have preceded these events, and identify practices your team can adopt to avoid them in the future.

PREPARING: COHERENCE BUSTING

The Trust Conversation is an exploration into unknown territory. You seek to understand your conversation partner's story, which you couldn't have known at first, and align your story with theirs. By contrast, the Fear Conversation is more directed; thanks to your work in the previous section, you will likely have some idea where there is normalization of deviance and you will be looking for fears underlying that normalization. The danger is that you can overdirect the Fear Conversation, focusing only on the fears and causes that seem likely from your point of view.

In this section, we're going to show you a technique we've developed for unlocking your inner curiosity and overcoming your assumptions: *Coherence Busting*. As a bonus, when applied to the examples of normalized deviance you found in the last section, this technique will give you a great head start on the Fear Chart you'll create in the Fear Conversation itself.

The Wrist Glance

To apply Coherence Busting, imagine yourself making a big proposal—one you really want to sell to your audience. While you are talking, you notice that the main stakeholder—the person you most hope to persuade—glances briefly at her wrist. What do you do? And why?

Before reading on, spend a minute or so making a short list of actions you might take and why you would take them in this situation. As you'll see in a moment, it's very important that you do not spend lots of time thinking about these actions; just jot down whatever comes to mind.

Done? Your responses almost certainly resemble one of these:

- I'll speed up, because she has somewhere else to go.
- I'll ask if I'm covering the right material, because she must be bored.
- I'll jump to my most persuasive slide, because she must be questioning my argument.

If your answers are anywhere close to these, congratulations! Your System 1 is in perfect working order—and it's likely to betray you in situations like this one.

System 1 and System 2

We introduce the wrist-glance scenario to let you experience the decision-making heuristics that Daniel Kahneman describes in his book *Thinking, Fast and Slow*. Kahneman models our consciousness as comprising two systems: our fast, automatic, unconscious System 1, and our slow, deliberate, effortful System 2.[8] Part of what makes System 1 fast is the shortcuts it uses. Two of these shortcuts consistently arise with the wrist-glance example. The first is that we assume that a coherent story must be correct. The second is that we limit the facts to what we can immediately recall, a process Kahneman calls, "WYSIATI," or "what you see is all there is."[9]

We unconsciously construct a coherent story for what the glance means—for instance, "She has somewhere else to go." This story is based on our first thought about what the glance might mean (WYSIATI). The coherence in our story gives us the sense that our story is true. We then design our actions in response to this story we made up, such as, "I'll speed up." This is the key lesson of the wrist-glance example: we feel like we are responding to the reality of the situation, because WYSIATI and coherence cause us to mistake our single plausible story for the truth. But often we are wrong—dangerously, catastrophically wrong. In fact, have a look back at our description of the wrist glance. We wrote that the stakeholder briefly glances at her *wrist*. We never mentioned a watch, but you almost certainly assumed there was one.

This is why we need Coherence Busting.

Busting the System 1 Story

Returning to the wrist-glance exercise, now consider other possible meanings of the wrist glance—*all* of the possible reasons: a nervous habit, an alert on her smartwatch, a rash on her hand, and lots more. Taking more time to think allows you to activate your System 2 and come up with a long list of possible reasons. This is Coherence Busting.

We find it particularly helpful to stretch yourself and even include wildly implausible explanations: she has her plan for world domination written on her hand, the glance is a hidden signal to members of her secret society, etc. In fact, we recommend you start your Coherence Busting with these extremely unlikely explanations because they are naturally humorous, and laughter is inherently incompatible with the fight-or-flight response you may be feeling as you consider the fear-based, dangerously coherent story that System 1 invented for you.

The key to Coherence Busting is not that there are lots of options but that the options are mutually incompatible. Once we can imagine conflicting explanations, we are no longer trapped by the original coherent story. These options were always there, but we needed System 2, our conscious and effortful thought process, to bring them to the surface. That's not something we do naturally when we feel we already have a good explanation, but it is vital to a successful Fear Conversation.

Applying Coherence Busting

You can use Coherence Busting to help you prepare any time you are approaching a potentially difficult conversation, especially when you sense that you may have some assumptions about how your conversation partner is thinking and feeling. (If you're like us, you almost always have assumptions like this!) In Table 4.2 (page 86), we've provided some examples of Coherence Busting in real situations.

When preparing for the Fear Conversation, Coherence Busting can help us take a more curious, open attitude into the discussion that will help us discover and mitigate fears we never would have imagined. To prepare, list as many fears as you can that might underlie each of the normalized deviances you came up with in the previous section. Be as broad as possible, engaging your System 2 to imagine fears that may seem unlikely or downright silly. You may want to put your ideas on sticky notes or index cards to help you develop the Fear Chart in the next section.

If you think:	Consider these alternatives:
My team is too lazy to write tests.	The CEO ordered all teams to stop testing. The team writes perfect code, so tests are superfluous. Someone told them tests are useless. They tried tests before and found them difficult.
Sales staff don't care about quality, only deadlines.	The Sales team is running a betting pool to see how ridiculous it can make the development targets. Salespeople believe code is always buggy, so quality doesn't matter. Deadlines are agreed to by executives, and Sales has no control over them.
Our database vendor knows we can't switch providers and is milking us for every penny it can.	A rogue executive is trying to destroy the company by driving away customers with ridiculous pricing. The pricing matrix has a typo in it, and we're actually due a substantial discount. Our account manager, knowing we're cash-strapped, negotiated a 50% reduction in the global rate increase.

Table 4.2: Coherence Busting in Action

Scoring for Coherence Busting

To score a Two-Column Conversational Analysis with Coherence Busting as the goal, look in your left-hand column and find as many unsupported conclusions as you can about others' thoughts or motivations. Look for signals like the words "obviously" or "clearly," as well as statements that don't have a firm basis in the right-hand column—for example, the assertion that the other person is denigrating your work without an explicit statement, like "I don't believe your project is up to scratch." To check if you've identified an unsupported conclusion, apply some Coherence Busting by trying to think up alternative explanations for the observations that led you to the conclusion; if you succeed in developing plausible substitutes, the conclusion must not be supported. Give yourself one point for each unsupported conclusion. Your goal should be to keep your score as low as possible.

The Conversation: The Fear Chart

With normalization of deviance and Coherence Busting under our belts, we're ready to have the Fear Conversation.*

Our first task in the Fear Conversation is to make all the fears we can think of *discussable*. This is where Coherence Busting will help—especially if the whole team has been able to do it. (If they haven't, consider introducing the idea of Coherence Busting at the start of the conversation, inviting everyone to take five minutes to engage their System 2 to generate ideas.) Then we will move on to filtering the key fears and, finally, mitigating those fears. You'll be constructing a Fear Chart as you go (Figure 4.1 at the end of this section, on page 90, shows how your chart might look at the end of this exercise).

> *Step 1.* Make visible all the fears identified so far (by you alone or by the whole team). We like sticky notes because you can move them around easily, but writing on a whiteboard or putting index cards on

---

* In this section, we're going to assume you're having the Fear Conversation with a group, such as the developers in a software team or group of managers in a larger organization. However, that's just to make our description easier to follow; you should feel just fine having the Fear Conversation with a couple of colleagues or with one other person. The methods we describe work equally well in a smaller group.

a table will work too. Solicit more fears from the group, perhaps by asking for more extreme versions of identified fears ("If a bug is bad, would an outage be worse?") or by asking for the opposite of identified fears ("We're afraid we'll lose staff. Are we also afraid of growing the team too fast?").

Step 2. Ask the group for more items to add or for ways to combine existing cards. Add new fears without editing them—our goal is to get all the ideas of the group identified, not to filter any out.

Almost always, some of the identified fears will reinforce each other and/or some will be completely incompatible. Reflect this by putting cards near each other or on top of one another, or by using labelled arrows to connect groups of cards, or use anything else that helps you see connections. Be sure you don't leave out quiet team members. Ask specifically whether a grouping is okay with those who developed it.

Step 3. Now it's time to filter the items that are worth pursuing and mitigating from those that we can safely live with. We like to use dot voting* to identify the fears that we want to mitigate, but you can use another method if you prefer. The more outrageous ideas that helped activate your System 2, such as those involving aliens or secret societies, will almost certainly not survive this process, having served their purpose in encouraging creativity. You will wind up with a subset of the fears that the group wants to deal with—those that are most concerning or most consequential.

Step 4. We'll achieve the goal of the Fear Conversation if we can identify mitigations that help us reduce each of the target fears. Mitigations may include things like:

---

* To use dot voting, tell the group that each person will have a few votes (we often use three or five, but any small number will work). Everyone comes to the board and makes a dot or tally mark next to one or more fears that he or she thinks is important to mitigate. Participants can allocate their votes as they please—they may use all their votes on one very important fear, split them, or vote just once for several fears—but their total votes must not exceed the number you allotted them at the start.

- Fear of buggy releases angering customers:
  - Discuss quality versus speed trade-offs with customers or their internal proxies, and agree to expectations.
  - Increase manual and automated testing coverage.
  - Agree with executives that they will handle any angry customers while the team improves quality.
- Fear of missing deadlines:
  - Understand deadline drivers and negotiate reduced scope or changed dates through conversation with Marketing or Sales.
  - Reduce scope with customer approval.
- Fear of failing to master new methods or technologies:
  - Define mastery and milestones on the way to successful mastery to show progress.
  - Increase training and learning opportunities.

List each fear, its mitigation, and (this is critical!) someone accountable for ensuring that you carry out the mitigation.

Step 5. Finally, if you like, add to the chart the espoused norm that corresponds to each soon-to-be mitigated fear to clearly display the expected positive result of the mitigation.

Figure 4.1 (see page 90) provides an example of what your completed Fear Chart might look like, but simply creating a Fear Chart isn't enough by itself; you'll need to ensure it is published (ideally, posted on a wall, though a wiki or other internal document store could also work) and discussed regularly, and that the mitigations are carried out. (See "the Accountability Conversation" in Chapter 7, for methods to ensure the latter.)

Creating a Fear Chart can be a transformational experience for a team, allowing them to discuss hidden concerns and address them effectively. But it isn't a once-and-done affair; you'll need to regularly revisit and revise your Fear Chart at least every six months as the team and its environment continue to evolve.

Now let's look at some examples of the Fear Conversation in action, starting with Tara's.

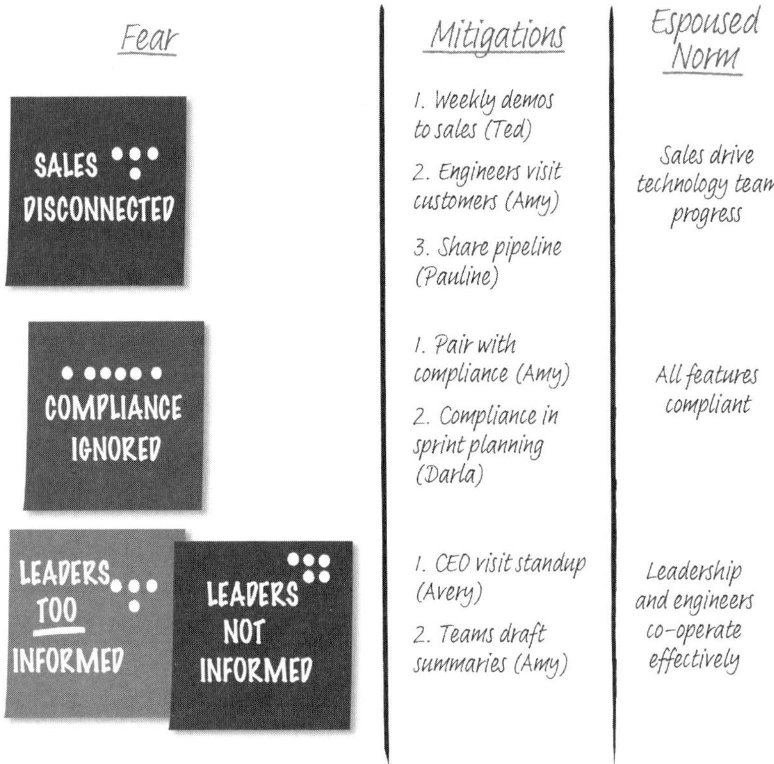

Figure 4.1: The Fear Chart

Tara's Fear Story Continued

Reflecting and Revising

Reflecting on my basic conversation scoring, I see I had five questions, but every one of them was leading, not genuine; I desperately wanted Matt to agree to something—anything—to get the key features done. I shared facts from the left-hand column early in the conversation but not my increasingly negative opinions about the developers and Matt. Matt's statement about yet another delay is an obvious trigger, and my pounding heart and nausea were very clear tells.

Scoring for Coherence Busting, I count five conclusions in my left-hand column, all unsupported. For instance, the developers might be blowing their targets but not because they are lazy; it might be because:

- They are secretly working for an evil supervillain bent on destroying our company.
- They don't understand the importance of the features.
- They don't have the experience to make good estimates.

Because I can come up with these alternative scenarios, I can see that my conclusion that "the developers are lazy" is unsupported. In fact, it's an example of defensive reasoning—I'm threatened by the potential delay, so I aim to "win" by blaming the engineers.

What can I do differently to Revise? Well, for one thing, I'm going to make a Fear Chart with Matt to help us discover and mitigate what's worrying us. I'm also planning to watch for conclusions in my left-hand column and try to think of other explanations for them. I've already started with the list above.

Improved Conversation

The Fear Chart conversation with Matt went really well, and we found that we shared a fear about not doing enough for customers, though we're not sure how to mitigate it yet. In last week's planning session, I decided to describe my fear when I felt it, so we could work on mitigations together.

Tara and Matt's Revised Conversation

What Tara thought and felt	What Tara and Matt said
Here we go again—another shortcut that we'll have to explain away.	Tara: Come on, you know that feature's only half of the story. Users can't even save their project at the end of the workflow!
I feel my chest pounding. What am I afraid of? I think it's that we'll have to postpone sales calls yet again, losing out on revenue.	Matt: Of course, but that's what we can do this sprint. We'll do the rest, including saving progress, in the next release.

We'll run out of money soon if we don't sell. And we can't sell like this. Why is this happening?

Tara: But we can't sell it as it is. Why do we say that we build valuable features when we never actually do?

Matt: I'm confused. I thought we built something useful every sprint. Identifying the value and building it is the purpose of these planning sessions, isn't it?

We always proclaim we give "value every sprint," but I think we've normalized our deviance from this principle.

Our team is larger than it used to be, but they're not working hard enough; or they have been hypnotized into working slowly, or they don't understand the features, or they need more training. Hmm, it seems there are lots of possible explanations for what I'm observing. I'll ask Matt's opinion to help us resolve this.

Tara: Well, they're not serving that purpose for me. I think we say we're building valuable increments, but for some reason, we keep making half-assed features that we can't sell. Why do you think that is?

Hmm, when I think about Matt's question, I keep coming back to the database project that consumed everyone's time for the whole summer. Maybe that's what's really scaring me.

Matt: That's tough to hear, Tara. Why haven't you said anything before now? I didn't know we were hurting sales by leaving out features. If you'd told me that, we could have made adjustments to get to at least some of them.

I feel enough trust in Matt to share my fear, now that I understand it myself.

Tara: That's a fair question. I think that I'm afraid that if I do, your team will go underground, like when they rebuilt the database and didn't release anything for months.

Matt: I didn't know that you felt that fear. We've learned a lot since the database build, and I'm sure we could do better now. For instance, could we skip step 7 and put in a working Save button instead? That would fit in the sprint.

This is what I wanted to discuss—trade-offs to increase the value.

This meeting could be productive after all.

Tara: Definitely!

Coherence Busting helped me at a crucial stage here, as I was able to avoid assuming the developers were to blame for slower progress by thinking of other explanations. It turns out that I was actually part of the problem. During planning, I wasn't always sharing my fear and explaining what effect I thought missing features would have on sales. (Look back at my first conversation with Matt. That fear is all over the left-hand column but never gets into the actual conversation on the right.) Now that we have this fear out in the open, I'm pleased to say that our planning sessions are much more effective, with useful discussions about changing scope to drive sales. And no more heart-failure close calls for me!

Example Fear Conversation

Tom and the Engineers: Fear of the Code

Tom says, "Ken was the technical lead and line manager, until I was brought in as people lead. I rapidly noticed that the release process seemed to be a source of bugs and annoyance, but nobody wanted to tell me exactly why—it seemed to be an undiscussable, fear-inducing topic. I decided to find out more in a session with Ken and the rest of the engineering team, first prompting them to think of fears related to releasing. I expected that this would help us uncover examples of normalization of deviance."

Tom, Ken, and the Engineers' Conversation

What Tom thought and felt	What Tom, Ken, and the engineers said
Let's make the current situation visible and discussable.	Tom: Okay, I think we've captured the release process on the board now. Are we missing anything?
I'm suspicious of the phrase "supposed to."	Dean: Yep, that's the process we're supposed to follow.
What do these important words mean?	Tom: What do you mean by "supposed to"?

Thoughts and Feelings	What Was Said
More problematic words—"of course"??	Ellie: Well, of course Ken doesn't follow it.
	Tom: Why "of course"?
Ah, this could be why everyone tiptoes around the problems with releases.	Ken: Ellie's right. I sometimes skip the code review and QA steps, and release straight to live.
Let's see if we can get to the underlying emotions.	Tom: Why is that? Is there a fear you can share that's driving this?
Good for you, Ken! When you told me about this fear yesterday, I hoped you'd be able to share it here.	Ken: There's lots of scary old code that only I understand. I guess I'm afraid that other people will get confused by it and make mistakes.
I can't argue with Frank here. But he hasn't told me or the others about this concern before.	Frank: That's unfair to us, Ken. We deserve to know how the whole app works. And besides, your unchecked releases cause bugs anyway.
	Tom: Frank, you haven't shared that opinion before—why is that?
Once again, an emotive phrase with many interpretations: "his code." I'm glad Frank can talk about this fear, though.	Frank: My fear is that Ken won't like it if we ask to look at his code.
Does Ken agree?	Tom: "His code," you said. Ken, do you see it as yours?
I think I may see a way to mitigate both fears.	Ken: Not at all. I'd like to share it, but I assumed everyone else wouldn't want to.
	Tom: I think it's fair to say Frank would like to share code ownership, right? Do others agree? I see lots of nodding.
Aha, this looks promising.	Ken: I'd be happy to work with others on the legacy code.
	Tom: And would that mitigate your fear of mistakes?

On the right track now!

Ken: For sure. I'll book a code review with Frank this afternoon.

Tom used the whiteboard to share the espoused norm—the process the team was "supposed to" follow. This helped the group to discuss how and why they had deviated from that norm, and what fears were driving that deviation. A Fear Conversation followed, after which it was much easier to create a Fear Chart to identify mitigations for those fears. Tom reported later that the team adhered much more closely to their espoused release process after this successful conversation.

CASE STUDY: OVERCOMING FEAR

Big Bang Twice a Year

"Four months," thought Thierry. "They'll never do it."

It was September 2018, and the Belgian Federal Pensions Service had just told Thierry de Pauw, a consultant to Agile teams, that its last major quarterly software release would be in December. After that, it would release new versions every two weeks, achieving "continuous delivery" and reducing cost and risk substantially.

With over 120 developers and a huge, fifteen-year-old application that calculated and paid pensions for every Belgian, the agency would have to change the ingrained habits of fifteen development teams, each of which made potentially interrelated changes to the monolithic code base. Every quarter, the build and release team would painstakingly merge all the changes from all the teams to produce a patched-together big-bang release of the application that was supposed to include everyone's new features. But since each team's code had been written in isolation, some of the pieces wouldn't work together. Stabilizing and delivering a working application took, they found, around 330 person days, a cost they could ill afford, and so they had decided the time had come to change.

And of course, as in many organizations, the quarterly releases weren't even quarterly; the intricate, highly manual release process usually led to missed deadlines and deployment delays, so the agency actually averaged more like two releases per year. The delays meant even more features had to be delivered in each new version, only adding to the complexity and risk.

In twenty years of leading software teams, Thierry had never seen any organization this large make the shift to continuous delivery this quickly. And the kicker was that the agency had hired him to help make it happen.

Finding the Fear

Using Joint Design (see the Why Conversation in Chapter 5 for more) with an ambitious "core team" of internal advocates for change, Thierry created value stream maps that captured the current process, all the way from the developer finishing the code to the feature going live in the application. These value stream maps helped the agency start identifying candidates for improvement. For example, the exercise revealed that there was a much faster "patch release" process occurring every two weeks; it was designed for quick fixes to existing features but was also occasionally and increasingly used for new functionality.

"Look at that!" he said, examining the value stream maps. "Amazing that they fit all their release processes into just two weeks for the patches." *This could lead to a smooth replacement of the old process with the new*, he thought, *with the next major release replaced by several small ones*.

But further investigation revealed the first of several fears that would threaten to block progress: *fear of complexity*. As they did for each release, the teams had created a variety of code "branches" (versions of the software that each contained a team's recent changes), with complex dependencies among them. Untangling this spaghetti into individual, releasable strands would require cherry-picking very carefully from multiple branches. This often went wrong when creating just one patch release, let alone a series of such releases that would capture six months of changes; the risk of error in making such a complex, midcourse adjustment was just too great. So, with a sigh, Thierry and the core team agreed to mitigate this fear by keeping to the plan for a major release in December. In January they would clear the branches and begin again with simpler, smaller units of functionality.

As they continued to work toward the new process, Thierry led the group in a series of Fear Conversations. Through this series of Fear Conversations, the team discovered several more fears: disengagement, skill gaps, missing key steps, deadlines, and bugs. We explore each in more detail next.

Fear of disengagement. The majority of the fifteen teams were working together to make continuous delivery happen, but a few were nowhere to be seen, doing little visible activity to get ready. Would they act in time? Would they refuse to join the new process? To mitigate this fear, the core team ensured that the steps to adopting the continuous-delivery model were simple and clearly documented; this way, it would be easy for the disengaged teams to catch up once they realized the changes were really going to happen. It helped that some of the late adopters were already heavy users of the patch-release process, as they would be able to adjust relatively quickly.

Fear of skill gaps. The new process would require changes be made in much smaller increments than before. Would the teams be able to adapt and break down their work into valuable changes that could be made in just two weeks? Thierry, having seen engineers deliver value daily at many other organizations, was not concerned about this—but his confidence made no difference. The teams needed a mitigation they themselves could believe in, and they got it by agreeing that they would have a safety net—a method of skipping a release with a feature branch if they failed to complete a change within the two-week time frame.

Fear of missing key steps. The long release process included a number of rituals, such as a code freeze and an all-team "go-no-go" decision meeting. Would these rituals be lost, and would the risk reduction they provided be lost as well? The mitigation here was relatively easy: the core team developed compressed versions of each ritual that could be carried out during the two-week release cycle, preserving their value while speeding up the overall process.

Fear of deadlines. As a part of the government, the agency had legally mandated deadlines; missing these was *not* an option. How could the team be sure they could hit these hard targets when the new process would be so compressed? Wouldn't a single failure derail the whole process? A fallback procedure worked to address this fear: near a hard deadline, the team could choose to release despite test failures *if* they devised sufficient work-arounds and mitigations.

> *Fear of bugs.* This was the greatest fear, especially for executives; a severe enough problem could land them on the front page of every newspaper in Belgium, damaging their reputation and costing the agency huge amounts of money to fix. And the fear was well founded: many automated tests were prone to false negatives, the tests often got out of sync with the code since they were stored separately, and manual testing was difficult to coordinate and organize. As a result, many bugs slipped past the testing process, and a large portion of the time for each major release was spent checking and rechecking the release candidate in an attempt to squeeze out all the bugs.
>
> "The major releases make people pay attention to quality and give us enough time to test," said the teams. "How could we possibly do enough checks in just two weeks to ensure no catastrophes will occur?" The core team invested heavily in addressing this fear by quarantining unreliable tests (failed tests were checked or mitigated manually), committing tests to the same repository as code to keep them synchronized, and planning manual testing more carefully with a focus on only the small set of changes in each two-week release.

Having mitigated each of these fears, and having made it through the final major December release, the core team got permission from the executives to roll out the new process. They entered 2019 with bated breath: Would their mitigations be enough? Would they be able to complete a full release just two weeks into the new year?

Smiles All Round

The answer was a resounding YES! The first release wasn't perfect, but it came out on time; and the core team was ready to address problems before the next one rolled around. The initially disengaged groups got involved, the teams figured out how to release partial changes rather than an entire feature, the compressed rituals worked and reduced risk, and the automated and manual testing procedures worked together to keep quality high and releases on time for deadlines. Making the fears discussable and then mitigating them had provided enough protection to let the agency make the first release as planned. And every two weeks after that, releases ran like clockwork.

Naturally, nothing is perfect, and the core team still had much work to do; a listening tour of the fifteen teams revealed that there were many fixes and improvements still required, but it also showed that the new process was universally welcomed, providing transparency across the organization. Thierry remembers one core team member who always looked sad during the run-up to the new process: "She was convinced the changes were needed but feared they would never happen. On my first visit after the initial release, her usual long face was replaced by a smile from ear to ear."

Conclusion: Applying the Fear Conversation

In this chapter, you learned about *identifying* fears using the clues provided by normalization of deviance; about *uncovering* fears that you may not see yourself using Coherence Busting; and about *mitigating* fears using the Fear Chart. By reducing your own and others' fears, you will help eliminate the threat, embarrassment, and defensive reasoning that interfere with conversational transformation. You can use the Fear Conversation in many ways, including the following:

- An ***executive leader*** can enable her organization to take more risks and identify more ways to remove obstacles to achieving company goals if a culture of psychological safety allows information about obstacles and risks to flow upward and downward effectively.
- A ***team lead*** can find out what options his team is not exploring during sprint planning, standups, or retrospectives, and what he can do to encourage more participation and creativity.
- An ***individual contributor*** can identify fears that are stifling her ability to adopt innovations, like Infrastructure as Code (IaC) or executable specifications, and with help from colleagues and managers, effectively mitigate those fears.

Chapter 5

The Why Conversation

So far, we have added tools to our conversational toolkit that can help us to build trust and reduce fear. These techniques address issues that prevent collaboration and reduce problem solving that might trap any team in the factory mind-set. Removing barriers to success was our first goal, but with the next tool, we begin the process of building up a positive framework for our team to work within. Building a Why gives our company a strategic direction that guides large and small decisions, and provides a strong motive for success. Independent decision-making and team motivation were not concerns in the noncollaborative factory, but they are vital once we break free of it and begin to operate autonomously.

Our central message in this chapter is that the Why you build must not only explain the impetus for your collective action as a team but be created *jointly*, with all those involved. An executive who imposes a Why from above—or worse, with only a sham consultation—does more harm than good. Jointly creating a purpose means that a chief architect can concentrate on pointing to the cloud as the next evolutionary step, that a tech lead can get her whole team behind the quarterly goal, and that a tester can decide with confidence which component she should automate tests for next.

When you finish working through these methods, you will be able to:

- Distinguish *interests* from *positions*, and uncover the former during a conversation that is stuck in an endless debate involving the latter.
- Combine *advocacy* and *inquiry* in a way that lets you be curious about the other person's view while transparently sharing your own.
- *Jointly design* a solution—such as a team Why—by using the previous two techniques together with clear decision-making and a timeboxed discussion, allowing all participants to be heard and yielding a result that everyone can say they contributed to.

Don't Start with Why

Simon Sinek, in one of the most-watched TED Talks ever, argues passionately that to be successful, organizations must always lead with their Why, the central reason for their existence and action. "What" and "How," the strategy and tactics that define their route to the Why, come later; to succeed, customers, employees, and investors need to first hear, understand, and align with the organization's purpose.[1]

In his talk and his follow-up book, *Start with Why*, Sinek cites a number of examples to support his argument:

- Explorer Ernest Shackleton, before attempting the first crossing of the Antarctic in 1914, reportedly advertised for people to join him thus: "Men wanted for hazardous journey. Small wages, bitter cold, long months of complete darkness, constant danger, safe return doubtful. Honour and recognition in case of success."[2]
- In a major rebranding in 1997, Apple's ads urged us to "think different," without mentioning their products at all. Establishing their company's mission so clearly with customers, and in a way completely divorced from their existing computer products, allowed them to dominate new categories in the following decade, such as music players, smartphones, and tablets.
- Dr. Martin Luther King Jr.'s inspiring 1963 speech described a vision of a new world where people would ". . . be judged not by the color of their skin but by the content of their character."[3] King had almost nothing to say about how his listeners would reach this promised land—and crucially, the speech was called "I Have a Dream," not "I Have a Plan."

Yet Dr. King managed to captivate and convince an audience of more than 250,000 people solely by talking about his beliefs.

In each case, a bold leader attracted followers and believers with a compelling argument for what the group was aiming to accomplish and achieved dramatic success, without dwelling on strategy or tactics. In our experience, a powerful Why also helps with a smaller, tactical change in just the same way.

It seems to follow naturally that if we want our team to scale similar heights, we need to share with them a genuine commitment to an inspiring Why. With a clear direction and internal commitment, they will be able to self-organize and succeed just like Shackleton, Apple, and King. Right?

With the utmost respect, we have to disagree. Starting with Why is dangerous and unlikely to succeed.

Yes, a clear purpose must be agreed upon if a team is to make productive use of techniques like iterative delivery and periodic reflection for improvement. And yes, alignment on this purpose must come before we can agree to scope, milestones, deadlines, targets, and everything else that we need to make the Agile engine go. That's the reason that the next two conversations, Why and Commitment, come in that order; and we will have a lot to say in both about how to build the internal commitment needed to align on the team's and the organization's Why.

Before the Why

But far too often, we have seen leaders try to inspire their teams without first having the Trust and Fear Conversations—and with dismal results. Without aligned stories that let everyone share a model of expected behavior, no one is ready to believe there is anyone steering the ship, much less believe there is anyone prepared to agree on a direction. And when unfettered fears dominate the team's thinking, they can't make room for the Joint Design of goals that forms the heart of the Why Conversation.

We're reminded of one team we worked with right after the launch of a software-as-a-service product that had taken nearly a year to build. Lack of iteration and customer involvement meant that the product was floundering, with salespeople unable to close even a single deal. Team members looked and felt demoralized, and no one seemed to know how to fix the software to make it marketable. It seemed obvious that what this group needed was a good dose of Sinek-style Why to help them re-engage with customers and iterate their way to a solution.

But when we dug deeper, we quickly found that there were underlying issues of trust and fear that meant this group was in no way ready for the Why Conversation. Leaders had made unilateral and unpopular decisions about team organization and product marketing. This had lead to badly misaligned stories about their motivation. And shortcuts like skipping code reviews and pushing features live without product owner involvement had led to understandable fears from the team about code and release quality. Trying to give this group an inspiring Why at this point would have been like Captain Bligh delivering a motivational speech to the crew of the *Bounty* just before the mutiny.

After lots of intense work with the organization, we unearthed a number of actions that helped to improve trust and mitigate fears, including:

- Redefining the team lead's role and coaching him in collaborative leadership, including making and fulfilling promises to include the whole team in decision-making.
- Making quality fears discussable and reshaping the release process to address them.
- Removing an ineffective senior leader whose actions had undermined trust.

Only after taking these actions was the team able to have a meaningful Why Conversation, discussing company and team goals and the reasons why the product launch had failed so badly, and then beginning the process of addressing missing features through iterative delivery (which is no longer a source of fear). The product is now selling briskly.

As you can see from this example, a team without a Why can be misaligned and directionless, while a powerful Why provides psychological safety and a clear alignment on goals. These techniques for jointly designing a powerful Why rely on a foundation of solid trust and reduced fears so that the team can work and build on the skills learned in the previous chapters, like Coherence Busting and TDD for People.

So ensure you've got those bases covered before proceeding. If you have, let's get started!

Bobby's Why Story

I'm Bobby, the team lead for a group in New York building the embedded software that runs inside an e-learning tablet for kids. Darius is my counterpart in hardware, building the tablet itself. Between us we're responsible for shipping new versions of the product, from chips to firmware to apps. The problem is that Darius is seven time zones away, so we almost never get to talk live. I think his team should shift their working hours so we overlap more. I woke up at the crack of dawn to discuss this with Darius on the phone, but the conversation went awry quickly. I've recorded it and will be analyzing it to find out what went wrong.

Bobby and Darius's Conversation

Reminder: read the right-hand column first, then go back and read right to left.

What Bobby thought and felt	What Bobby and Darius said
Surely, you'll see the benefits of increasing communication.	*Bobby: We've got to get more overlap between the teams. Would you be willing to start and finish later to make that work?*
Well, stonewalling isn't going to get us anywhere.	*Darius: No, that won't be possible.*
I don't think Santa Claus is going to shift his delivery date for us. Our mission is to make kids happy and smart; missing Christmas would achieve neither!	*Bobby: Huh?! But our communication has to improve. The product has to be ready on time for Christmas, and the delays are killing our plan.*
I can't believe this. Our documents are perfectly clear! His engineers just don't want to read them.	*Darius: You don't understand. Staying late won't fix the delays when the problem is bad documentation.*
I'll try again to make the case.	*Bobby: If it is documentation that's at fault—and I don't think it is—how can we ever find out where it's wrong if we don't talk more?*

I agree, talking to you won't help. You make a brick wall look transparent!	Darius: It won't help. If we get good specs, we can build to them. That's the only way.
I'm out of options. I can't do anything when you're digging in your heels.	Bobby: I give up. If you won't move your working hours voluntarily, I'll have to ask our CEO to make you do it.

Darius is terse and uncommunicative in email and chat, but I thought he'd open up on the phone. Boy, was I wrong! He's even more stubborn in real life. Seems to me that we don't agree about the causes of delays or how to communicate better, or even why we're making these tablets in the first place. I don't see how I can work with Darius at all.

PREPARING: INTERESTS, NOT POSITIONS; ADVOCACY PLUS INQUIRY

Your purpose in the Trust and Fear Conversations was to uncover and make discussable previously hidden ideas (stories and fears, respectively). You might imagine that the Why Conversation will be easier, because you can just tell your colleagues all the inspiring reasons that their work is important. Right?

Sadly, that's very unlikely to work, because odds are that your inspiring reasons are not going to be meaningful to some or all of the rest of the team. We know of one executive in the banking industry who spent years telling everyone that his company existed to make markets efficient. That was true, and the company was indeed very successful at removing financial inefficiencies; but this Why made exactly zero impact on product design, hiring, or employee motivation, because it just didn't matter to most software developers and product managers working there.

Instead, we are going to suggest you do something much harder: *jointly design* the Why for your organization. This is harder than it seems, because it means negotiating and compromising, one step back and two steps (we hope) forward—a seeming waste of time. It's also harder because it means the death of the ego for all sides; we can no longer believe that we are the only source of truth and direction in our working lives. It's especially difficult for executives or founders who sincerely believe that they are the only ones who know, or should know, the right direction for the organization. But Joint Design is the only way to create internal commitment and self-organization in a team.*

We will describe Joint Design itself in the next section, but before that, we have two specific techniques to offer: *Interests, Not Positions* and *Combining Advocacy and Inquiry*. Both are useful in any situation where you need to collaborate with others in an area of contention.

Interests, Not Positions

Arthur Martirosyan, a negotiator for the humanitarian organization Mercy Corps, tells the story of a successful negotiation using the "interests, not positions" technique from the book *Getting to Yes: Negotiating Agreement without Giving In*:[4] An oil company discovered large new reserves in postwar Iraq and prepared to begin drilling immediately. Unfortunately, the oil lay directly under fields being tilled by tenant farmers, who were not ready to give up their crops. Even more unfortunately, their threats to arm themselves and shoot up the company's office were completely credible in a society still recovering from a civil war and riven by sectarian violence. This seemed to be an intractable standoff, with neither side willing to give up their *positions*: the oil company wanted to drill, and the farmers wanted to farm. Stalemate!

However, Martirosyan detected an opportunity to refocus the discussion on each side's *interests*: he observed that the oil wasn't going anywhere, but the farmer's harvest was near at hand.

Could the oil company wait a short time to take over the land? *Yes*, as their interest was in protecting their claim and exploiting the resource for many years to come.

Could the farmers harvest and then leave? *Yes*, as their interest was in selling the crops they had worked hard to plant and to grow.

The resolution was obvious as soon as the conversation shifted to interests: the crops matured, the farmers harvested, and *then* the drills moved in, right after the tractors left. Some of the farmers even got jobs on the oil field!

Difficult conversations in your organization are unlikely to involve evicting tenants or dodging (literal) bullets, but your colleagues may have positions that

* In addition, you'll likely need to renew your Why periodically, as team members come and go and the environment changes. All the more reason to become skilled at the Why Conversation!

are just as entrenched as those of the oil company and the farmers, if not more so. It's important to try to identify these positions ahead of any difficult conversation, as well as some thoughts on possible corresponding interests. (Don't forget your *own* positions and interests!) As usual, enlisting the help of someone from outside the organization can often help you in identifying these, as *you* may be blind to them.

Table 5.1 provides some examples of positions and their corresponding interests.

Position	Possible Corresponding Interests
We must release feature X this quarter.	Keeping up with competitors Delivering on customer promises Protecting reputation for on-time delivery
We must eliminate our technical debt.	Delivering quality products Keeping developers happy Recruiting new technical staff
We have to stop buffering incoming feature requests.	Increasing delivery predictability Improving team throughput Keeping up with industry practices
We need to use containers to deploy.	Reducing deployment failures Diagnosing production problems faster Learning about new technology
We need a system of salary grades.	Ensuring equitable employee treatment Avoiding lawsuits Retaining staff
We have to fire Jane.	Resolving performance issues quickly Reinforcing our culture and values Reducing the staff budget

Table 5.1: Positions and Possible Interests

Distinguishing positions and interests during conversations can often help you and the rest of the group avoid getting stuck in unending and fruitless debate.* If you see hardened and opposing positions emerging, or if you feel your position is becoming immovable, aim to identify and share the reasoning and the interests that led to these positions.

For instance, two of three startup founders were arguing vigorously over what sales strategy to adopt—one passionately in favor of expanding within existing customers, the other just as firmly espousing opening additional markets with new products. The third founder watched in silence for a while, until we invited her to interject. At this point, she drew a chart on the whiteboard that illustrated a new way of understanding the interests of the other two founders (see Table 5.2). By introducing the vertical axis, she made it possible for all of us to see that there was a shared interest in offering a mix of options to existing and new customers, ranging from known and loved features to totally new ones, born from research. The debate shifted to the much more productive topic of what this mix was currently and what it should be.

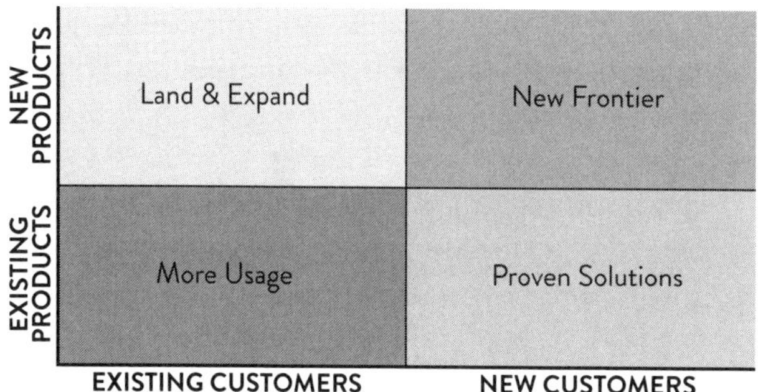

Table 5.2: Product Insights

To prepare for the Why Conversation specifically, try to create a table like Table 5.1, where the positions are specific team or organization goals that you

* Remember the Ladder of Inference from the Trust Conversation (page 61)? A battle that is position-based like this often involves lots of action advocacy from the top of the ladder, without any sharing of the reasoning (including the *interests*) that led to the differing conclusions. We have heard this aptly called "dueling ladders."

think colleagues may advocate, and the interests describe the broader principles that may be behind their advocacy.

Combining Advocacy and Inquiry

As we noted in Chapter 2, our natural tendency is toward unilateral control and vigorous advocacy; we believe that if we just tell others what our views are, they will be forced by logic and our brilliant rhetoric to agree with us (since we are right anyway). Argyris tells us that paying attention to our conversations will help us unlearn this habit,[5] and methods like TDD for People and Interests, Not Positions lead us away from this one-sided advocacy toward transparency and curiosity. We are not the only ones with the truth; and asking genuine questions will help us understand how others see the situation, allowing us to come up with new solutions together.

But there are dangers in tilting too far toward pure inquiry. Consider how one of us approached a conversation with a colleague, Sergiusz, about how to get user input on a new report. Because both Jeffrey and Sergiusz did conversational analyses, we have access to the thoughts of *both*—a unique *three*-column conversational analysis. Sergiusz and Jeffrey wrote down the conversation together, and thus, both of their thoughts were recorded (Sergiusz's is in the left-hand column and Jeffrey's is in the right-hand column). What was actually said appears in the middle column.

Sergiusz and Jeffrey's Conversation

Note: read the center column first.

What Sergiusz thought and felt	What Sergiusz and Jeffrey actually said	What Jeffrey thought and felt
I think we should have a follow-up meeting with Rob, but I don't think it is useful to pursue others.	Sergiusz: I think we should send the analysis to Rob. His comments will tell us whether we're building the right thing.	I'm not sure about that. I think he's got a lot of interest in the topic, but he's just one stakeholder among many.
Hmm, okay. Let's see where this is going.	Jeffrey: What makes you say that?	Maybe there's something I don't know. I wasn't part of earlier meetings with Rob's team.

I think he manages the users who are going to read the report.	Sergiusz: Because I got the impression that his team runs similar reports, and he'll know what they should look like.	I don't think he is a manager; just an interested and vocal user.
This is turning into a duel, not a discussion. I don't think these are genuine questions.	Jeffrey: Well, there are others who are interested too. Who is the report for?	I suspect there's an executive above Rob who makes the real decisions. I'm not sure you have enough understanding to start building. I'll test my understanding and make sure we are aligned on the customer and the goal first.
I really don't think this is the issue we should be discussing. We just need to get feedback, not relitigate the purpose of the report.	Serguisz: It's for operational managers, the ones keeping the system running smoothly.	I'm confused and a bit concerned. What problem do you think they are solving?
I don't agree. But maybe if you score this point, we can get on with deciding how to get feedback.	Jeffrey: Nope, it's for the business sponsor, the one who controls the budget. What will she do as a result of getting the report? Why are we building it in the first place?	Are you just making stuff up? You don't seem to understand the customer need at all.
This is really going off the rails. Why are you cross-examining me? Are you trying to make me look bad? I wish I could escape to a meeting, or a root canal or something.	Serguisz: I'm not sure. It might not lead her to do anything differently.	She'd do nothing differently? Why would we build it then?? I think we are really misaligned here. This is a great chance to make sure we're on the same page. Good thing I can spend some more time with you on this.

As you can see, although Jeffrey thought he was working toward a mutual understanding of the situation by presenting a series of questions, Sergiusz felt he was being "led down the garden path," and became increasingly concerned that Jeffrey had a hidden agenda. The conversation had a completely unintended effect: instead of increasing mutual learning, it led to mistrust and fear for Sergiusz.

We call this the *Perry Mason Trap*. When we ask a series of questions without explaining our reasoning or stating our views behind these questions, we run the risk that our conversation partner will think we are—like the twentieth-century TV lawyer—leading up to some unpleasant surprise. ("Aha! So you admit you drive a bright pink sports car—*just like the one seen speeding away from the scene of the crime!*")

To avoid this trap, aim to combine advocacy of your own position with inquiry about that of your conversation partner, as espoused by Peter Senge in *The Fifth Discipline: The Art & Practice of the Learning Organization*.[6] This takes a lot of practice to do skillfully, so here are some example approaches to achieving this difficult combination:

- "It seems to me that we have to cut the hiring budget to match these reduced revenues. Do you see this differently? For example, are there any other areas we could look at cutting, or is making cuts the wrong way to respond?"
- "I wonder how many different ways we can offer this product. I've thought of two—on the home screen and as an add-on at checkout. What other ideas can you think of?"
- "I hear some of our client implementations are behind schedule, and I'm wondering if we should delay some of them. You're closer to the delivery teams; how do you see the situation? And what solution would you suggest?"

A fortunate side effect of combining advocacy and inquiry is that you also remind yourself to include your own observations and ideas in the conversation, sharing your Ladder of Inference—something that is surprisingly easy to forget once you start aiming for greater mutual learning. Once you've managed to be transparent about your own view and curious about the other persons' ideas, you are well on your way to mining much more value from your conflicts.

PREPARING: JOINT DESIGN

Adding Your Own Egg

Soon after the invention of cake mix, one of its early manufacturers* noticed a problem: *many housewives*† *refused to buy it. This is odd,* its executives thought; *why would anyone prefer the messy process of measuring and sifting and stirring when they could just add water to some powder from a box?*

This had the company stumped for a while, until someone had the bright idea to actually *ask* some customers. They discovered that the cake mix method was *too easy*—it didn't feel like baking if there was only one step to follow. Customers wanted to feel proud of making their family something sweet and delicious; but with the mix, they weren't involved. They felt like they might as well have gone to the bakery and bought one of the cakes off the shelf.[9]

The solution was obvious: remove the powdered egg, and require the customer to break and stir in an honest-to-goodness real egg. The phrase "add your own egg" on the front of the box‡ gave enough involvement and agency to the customer to make the process feel like real baking again, and sales shot up.§

Baking a Better Decision

We often see teams trying to make decisions—about process, or estimation, or tooling, or budget, or even who sits where—in a centralized, nonconsultative way. Leaders pursuing efficiency and correctness make fundamental decisions and then communicate them to the team, expecting enthusiastic adoption of the new plan. All too often, as with the cake-mix customers, the reaction

---

* While it is typically assumed to be Duncan Hines, the latest research suggests that P. Duff and Sons of Pittsburgh were actually the first to make this realization.[7]

† Apologies for our gendered language. This was in the mid-twentieth century, when most cake bakers were, indeed, housewives; and this was how marketers talked about their customers at the time.[8]

‡ For an example of this on an old cake-mix box, visit https://www.thissheepisorange.com/office-psychology-let-your-people-add-an-egg/.

§ Though the story is well known, we are indebted to Gerald Weinberg's *Secrets of Consulting* for this version, and the memorable phrase "add your own egg."[10]

is decidedly less positive, with reluctant compliance at best or flat refusal at worst. And of course, this is catastrophic when it involves the most fundamental decision of all: the definition of the team's motivating Why.

Instead, for decisions big and small, use the process of Joint Design, with each member of the team "adding their own egg." Here is the process:

- Include as many people as possible.
- Ask genuine questions (see Chapter 2).
- Invite opposing views.
- Timebox the discussion.
- Establish and communicate who will make the final decision (known as a *decision-making rule*[11]).

First, observe that the techniques of the previous section—Interests, Not Positions and Combining Advocacy and Inquiry—will be very useful in your Joint Design discussion. When you ask genuine questions, listen for and inquire about the interests behind the answers you hear. And when you invite opposing views, remember to also advocate appropriately. If you can do this, even with only partial success, you will be helping everyone provide useful information and feel like part of the decision.

Notice a Joint-Design process doesn't need to be the same as a democratic or consensus-driven one. The decision rule can mean that there is no need for everyone to agree with the decision, or even for most of the group to endorse it; and the timebox—the fixed amount of time set for the discussion—ensures that we won't get bogged down in endless debate. The key elements are *inclusion* ("I was part of the decision, and my objections were heard") and *information flow* ("I was able to share what I know"). Over and over, we see that we make better decisions and earn meaningful internal commitment when we follow this process.

Scoring for Joint Design

To score a Two-Column Conversational Analysis for Joint Design, look at the five elements listed above and award yourself a point for each one you can observe in your discussion. Did you include everyone who was relevant and available? Did you pose genuine questions and encourage views that don't match yours? And was the conversation limited both by an agreed time limit and by a decision-making rule? Scoring five of five means you succeeded in making a decision that is likely to have everyone's internal commitment.

Joint Design for Every Taste

There are many flavors of Joint Design. We've seen it used in groups of two and groups of two hundred, in short meetings and over many weeks, with small and large decisions. To illustrate just one variety, consider the fifteen-person engineering team we worked with whose release process was error prone and slow. Everyone agreed some automation and discipline would help, and we had a pretty good idea what an improved process might look like. It would have been easy to simply design a new deployment protocol and implement it.

Instead, remembering the cake-mix lesson, we gathered the team together and drew the current process on a whiteboard, marking the areas of friction and inefficiency in red. We set a timer and made this announcement:

"This is today's release process, and here are the bits you've told us aren't working well. For the next twenty minutes, we'll listen to any and all proposed changes; and using this eraser and pen, we'll update the steps accordingly. When the timer goes off, we're going to publish whatever is on the board as our new release process and ask all of you to try it. If it's a disaster, we'll buy everyone a beer in two weeks. Who wants to start?"

Ideas flew in from all sides, including several we wouldn't have thought of, making use of tools we didn't know about and contextual information from several specialties like QA and system administration. Further, it turned out we hadn't understood the existing process correctly, and we had to add a few steps to our diagram to make it work at all. In just a few minutes, we had a much better design on the board than we would have come up with by ourselves—and everyone in the room felt like they were part of that design. They enthusiastically implemented the new system—which was indeed smoother and less buggy than the old one—and we didn't have to buy anyone a beer.

We believe "adding your own egg" is vital to successfully determining your team's motivating Why. Now let's see how that works.

The Conversation: Building a Why

How do organizations normally define their purpose, decide their strategy, or start on a major transformation? In our experience, it's typically a task addressed by a board of directors, a small group of leaders, or just a couple of executives. They retreat in some way (to a boardroom or an off-site location), argue and debate and cogitate, and return to present a mission statement or a roadmap or a values definition. Then the rest of the company is expected to applaud politely and return to work.

If you've been paying attention to the last few sections, you probably won't be surprised that we are very skeptical about this approach. For one thing, the deciding group is probably lacking important information held by those outside it, so their decision will very likely be deficient in important ways. Also, and perhaps even more importantly, the rest of the organization will have little or no investment in the decision, so it will be easy for them to ignore it or pay it no more than lip service—hardly a motivating, vigorously championed Why.

The problem is that there's no obvious practical alternative to the dreaded off-site meeting. Should the group vote on its mission? Discuss until a consensus emerges? Pick options from a hat? With more than two or three people in the organization, these rapidly become unwieldy and inefficient options.

That's why we advocate a Joint Design approach to the Why Conversation, whether your team is tiny or huge, as we outlined above. Be as inclusive as you can. Invite alternative views, and combine advocacy and inquiry using genuine questions. Establish a decision-making rule and (if appropriate) limit the time for the discussion.

What does this look like? Well, consider one of our clients, who embarked on a Why Conversation to set new guiding values after a significant expansion. The organization established the overall goal of resetting company direction for their new growth phase and explained the business drivers behind the planned expansion. Then they made a significant effort to poll everyone for their views—no small feat for a small HR team covering several offices with new staff—resulting in a list of over one hundred value ideas, with more than 60% employee participation. Smaller groups then discussed and debated the values, with facilitators asking questions and ensuring everyone's views were heard. After a set period for this discussion, the board met, reviewed the leading ideas, and selected three values for the company, which were enthusiastically received.

At the same time, two product managers who worked closely together within the company were reshaping their own Why. Until we met them, the two had functioned as order takers within what amounted to a feature factory (see Chapter 1), transmitting requests from executives to the developers with little or no filtering or feedback. With gentle encouragement and lots of genuine questions, we helped them discover that they wanted to take a much more directive role.

Interestingly, by involving developers and stakeholders and listening for the interests of each, they found that more filtering and product direction was exactly what their teams and their managers wanted too. It only took a week or two for them to begin using their new purpose to define and focus on a new product direction. Combined with the overall renewal of values and purpose in the company Why, the clearer product and personal Why for the PMs resulted in a much faster cycle time, dramatically increased customer feedback, and the launch of a new product in less than a month.

Bobby's Why Story Continued

Reflecting and Revising

Time to Reflect by scoring my conversation with Darius. I had two questions, but they were both leading rather than genuine, as I was trying to get him to adopt my position that we should shift working hours. I didn't share my negative views about Darius and his team, even when I got really frustrated at the end. And I really react badly when I think someone is ignoring me or shutting down, as Darius seemed to early on; that's either a twitch or a trigger that I should watch out for.

Turning to Joint Design, I can give myself a point for timeboxing, since the inconvenient hour provided a natural stop to the discussion. But I don't get any other points: I could have included other members of Darius's team; I already noted I didn't ask genuine questions; I ignored Darius's opinion about documentation completely; and we certainly didn't have an agreed decision-making rule, since I felt I had to escalate to the CEO in the end. One out of five isn't very good.

To Revise my conversation, I'd definitely like to be more curious and find out what Darius's views really are. We might be able to come up with something better if I could just get him to open up; avoiding my tendency to shout when I think I'm being shut down should help. It would also be useful to understand what motivates him—for instance, why is he so firmly opposed to increasing communication?

Improved Conversation

I flew out to see Darius, figuring we'd have a better conversation face to face. On the plane, I worked to Role Play both sides of the conversation with my revisions in place. On arrival, I tried to involve other people from Darius's team in our discussion, but he told them not to come. I was worried we'd have another fight and my journey would be wasted.

Bobby and Darius's Revised Conversation

What Bobby thought and felt	What Bobby and Darius said
This seems pretty obvious to me, but let's be sure Darius sees the problem as I do.	Bobby: Darius, would you agree we've had some problems coordinating hardware and software?
Okay, we agree something isn't right.	Darius: Certainly—we still haven't been able to release the new product after three months.
I'm going to share my position so we can discuss it.	Bobby: Indeed. For a long time my position has been that we need to talk more.
That's what I keep hearing from everyone over here. Why on earth is it difficult?	Darius: I know, but you don't seem to understand that this is very difficult for us.
	Bobby: Is it the time difference that makes it tough?
Ah. I didn't realize the team sees language as the barrier. He's right that their English is poor, but I thought they wanted to improve. I bet this is why he didn't have them come along to this meeting.	Darius: Not really. We can and often do work to your schedule. But most of us, except me, speak very little English.
Let's be sure I've got Darius's position clear.	Bobby: So your position is that we should avoid in-person discussions? Does that include bringing others to this meeting?

What I'm thinking and feeling	What I'm saying
Not the first time I've heard this.	Darius: Yes. There's no point in us trying to talk more if we can't understand you. Just send us the detailed specifications and we'll build them.
Let's try to get to the interest behind Darius's position.	Bobby: That's what we've been trying, but it doesn't seem to be working. Tell me, why do you say "send the specs"? What good result would come from doing that?
Great, I definitely share that interest.	Darius: We could get on with our hardware build, as efficiently as possible.
	Bobby: I can't argue with that. It seems like we both have a strong interest in efficiency. Is that right?
She sure is efficiency focused—it was her idea to hire in this country, so hardware designers would be near the factory.	Darius: Certainly. Our CEO talks about nothing else, it seems.
I have a sneaky idea. Would it work for Darius?	Bobby: Hmm. Would it be more efficient if the specs were easier to read?
Sounds like better specs would indeed be more efficient.	Darius: Of course. We waste a lot of time over here debating what the requirements mean. But how would we do that?
We might have to stick to written communication, but with a translator, we could eliminate a big barrier to understanding.	Bobby: Well, I was thinking of hiring a technical translator to convert the documents into your language.
Oh, that sounds promising for my interests too.	Darius: I like that! The translator could help us understand you on video calls too.
	Bobby: I hadn't thought of that, but it's a great idea. Shall we write a job ad together?

We turned out to have a common interest in efficiency—our shared Why is building the product efficiently. Once we focused on this, we found a creative solution to the communication challenges that addressed both of our interests. The translator is helping us a lot now, and we also found a new engineer who speaks the hardware team's language—and she's teaching the rest of us to speak it too.

Example Why Conversations

Theresa and the Tech Team: Choosing a Focus

Theresa says, "I'm the newly hired engineering leader for a team that's frankly been way off track for some time. The company needs them to start delivering to business priorities, and I need their internal commitment to a new direction.

"I decided to call a Why Conversation meeting with developers and product managers to agree on and jointly design the way forward."

Theresa and the Tech Team's Conversation

What Theresa thought and felt	What Theresa and the team said
I'll lay out the ground rules to start: I need information flow from everyone, and a clear decision at the end.	Theresa: Thanks for coming, everyone. We're going to spend the next hour setting our team direction. I expect everyone to participate and propose ideas, but I may step in to make a decision if needed. At the end of the hour, whatever is on this whiteboard will be our direction for the next month. Everyone got that?
	Engineers: Yes, we've got it.
	PMs: Okay.

Let's get the team involved from the start in setting the topics.

Theresa: Okay, working with the PMs, I've prepared these sticky notes describing various items we might work on. First, have a look at all of them and tell me if any are not worth even examining. And if any important ones are missing, add your own sticky note.

Good point. Glad he's participating.

Patrick: We forgot single sign-on.

Theresa: Go ahead and add it. Any others?

I agree, but I might be missing something, especially since I'm new to the team.

Quentin: Test automation is up there, but shouldn't it be a routine part of coding, not a project?

Advocacy and inquiry seem to be working here.

Theresa: I tend to agree, but what do others think? I see nods, so I'm removing it. Other thoughts?

Nice observation. Glad she's engaging.

Roberta: There are three usability changes that are almost the same.

Let's move on to categorization.

Theresa: That's a good observation. Let's group them together under the heading "usability." What other categories make sense?

[Over the next few minutes, six categories emerge.].

No more than three areas with this small team—that's a limit that I want to set clearly. It sure seems to me that we need usability improvements to stop customer churn, but I'm genuinely interested in other ideas.

Theresa: I want to focus on just three of these for the next month, given our limited capacity. I see usability as vital but don't have a strong opinion about the other two. Which three would you pick? I'm especially interested to hear from you if you disagree with me.

Sam: I'd take automation, onboarding imports, and pricing simplification. All three reduce costs for operations.

Roberta: Why not usability?

	Sam: Easy—no cost reduction.
I'm curious here. Is there a strong reason for reducing cost that I don't know about?	*Theresa: What do others think? Is cost our driving consideration this month?*
That's how I see it; I wonder if anyone disagrees?	*Patrick: I don't think so. It's important, sure, but we need revenue more.*
Hmm. We just raised a million dollars. I'm not sure this is right.	*Sam: We always need to conserve cash. The company can't run on fumes.*
	Roberta: The CEO said yesterday that we need to land prospects, and we all know prospects convert when they aren't frustrated by poor usability and too many clicks.
Time to make a ruling and keep us on track.	*Theresa: This is a good debate, and I'm glad we are having it. I'm going to step in and say—sorry Sam!—that pure cost-reduction initiatives like automation have to be out this month. [I removed the automation sticky notes.] We're after new sales first, and we're willing to put up with some uncomfortable costs to get them.*
	Quentin: What about imports? Those help convert customers, and at the same time, they make setup a lot smoother for operators.
	Theresa: Very good point! What do you think, Sam?

Theresa continued in this way throughout the hour; and though not everyone agreed at the end, they all understood the Why behind the choices the group had made. All were willing to work toward the three focus areas left on the board and understood, even if they still disagreed, why the others had been left out for now. Theresa had used genuine questions combined with advocacy and inquiry to ensure information flowed freely and everyone got to participate. The time limit and decision-making rule stated at the beginning guaranteed a timely decision. The team was ready to build!

Terrence, Barry, and Victor: Changing Product Direction

Terrence says, "I'm the product manager for our line of casual online games. I've just presented a new plan for developing new games to the executive team, and the CEO and chief designer, Barry and Victor, have stayed in the room to talk with me further. This doesn't bode well . . ."

Terrence, Barry, and Victor's Conversation

What Terrence thought and felt	What Terrence, Barry, and Victor said
I thought you told me to make the process simpler!	Victor: We shouldn't be automating the process of developing new games!
I didn't expect Barry to agree. This is serious.	Barry: Yes, your plan is going to endanger playability and quality.
I'm going to try to find my feet here by advocating while inquiring.	Terrence: Slow down—I'm confused. I thought a simpler product-design experience would help us iterate better. Am I missing something?
	Victor: Of course we want a better design process, but not a button that deploys the whole game in one go.
I'll keep inquiring. What is their interest?	Terrence: I'm still confused. The games don't go live to real customers, only internally. Doesn't that help us test and improve faster?
Aha, that's the issue.	Barry: Yes, but part of the process that's important to us is storyboarding and experimenting offline. Your button is going to encourage the artists and coders to commit to code and designs too early.
I didn't realize the designers wanted to work offline.	Terrence: I get it. So the current process is slower than it could be, but you value that slowness.

Victor: Right. In the early stages we need to get the feel of the game.

Barry: Once we've approved it creatively, then we can speed up and automate.

Terrence: I think I see. We share an interest in eliminating the rote work involved in deploying a new game, but the initial creative steps need to remain offline and reflective.

Let me check my new understanding. They do want automation but for operators, not designers—right?

Victor: Exactly. What differentiates us is that we take time to design, unlike the competition, who slam out two or three crappy games a week.

Barry: I'll be the first to say that we should be reducing cost and delay. But not by cutting out fun and originality.

That's it. I missed the need for offline work, but I was right about the value of automation.

Terrence: I definitely agree about emphasizing quality over quantity. Could we use the new deployment mechanism, but only in Operations, not Creative?

Okay, let me try out a solution here. Does this match our new alignment on where automation makes sense?

Victor: Fine with me. Just don't let the designers anywhere near it.

Barry: The automation would save a lot of wasted effort by system administrators running scripts, right?

Barry gets it—cost savings without compromising quality.

Terrence: Exactly. I'll have a revised plan to you this afternoon.

Terrence thought he and the executives were aligned on their Why but found out suddenly that this wasn't the case. He focused on common interests and kept combining advocacy and inquiry, eventually discovering the source of the misalignment. The three were then able to realign with a common understanding of the proper place for automation in their game design process.

CASE STUDY: STUCK ON WHY

The Sea of Knowledge

Michelle was swimming in oceans of data. After several years at a small startup, with only a few customers, she'd joined a team working on one of the largest marketplaces in the world, with millions of users around the globe. As a product manager, she felt she'd died and gone to heaven. No more coaxing users into research sessions or releasing new features on a hunch and a prayer; now she could simply dip into the data and locate improvement opportunities based on the actual clicks and purchases of real, paying users.

In the first few days after her weeklong orientation, she began investigating the wide variety of products offered. As you'd expect in a widely used retail service, a few "whale" products were wildly popular, while a "long tail" of much less sought-after items were rarely bought individually but dwarfed the whales in aggregate. She categorized and queried the product database over and over as patterns and hypotheses began to emerge.

At the same time, she got to know her team, a small group of seasoned engineers. Though she'd only known them for a short time, she could tell that they were tight-knit and functioning well, with high trust and low fear. In fact, despite the very high visibility of their service, she was amazed to see them bravely making substantial changes to core components like the recommendation engine, willing to run an experiment and roll it back right away if it didn't work. "This is my kind of place," she thought. "I can really make some improvements fast."

An Unexpected Challenge

One hypothesis jumped out at Michelle from the results of nearly every query she ran: she was sure that many of the products had to be duplicates. After all, they were being entered by ordinary users with only simple validations, and surely one person's "red" would be another's "burgundy" or "cherry." It was hard to confirm this from queries in the local, aggregated database; she'd need an engineer to write and run a function on a large server farm to check her guess on the real petabyte-sized data set. But if it were true, it would unlock many opportunities to combine products and boost sales substantially, with much more effective marketing and recommendations. She confidently headed over to the engineers' desks.

"Hey Alan," she said to the developer who, since he was eating lunch, looked most interruptible. "I'd like to run a large query to look for duplicate products. Here's what I've been doing locally. Can you put the request on your backlog and run it, say, later this week?"

Alan stopped chewing and regarded Michelle skeptically. "Why?" he asked.

"Well," she replied, "if we can combine identical products, the recommendations will be—"

"That's not what I asked," he said. "I asked 'Why?'"

"I'm trying to tell you. Once we know what's duplicated, we can combine them and—"

He waved his pizza at her and she stopped, confused. "I don't think you're listening to me. I want to know why we should investigate duplicates."

"Because if we know about them, we can fix them! Isn't that obvious?"

"No," he said, "it isn't. I'm not going to work on this until you can tell me why it's worth doing." And with that, he took a final bite, opened his editor, and began typing, the conversation clearly over.

Michelle was shocked. She'd never been challenged so directly by a developer before. But when she thought about it, she had to say he could be right. She really couldn't say exactly why fixing duplicates was more valuable than what Alan was doing at the moment; it just seemed right to her. She resolved to find out and give him a convincing Why.

Why Wins the Day

Michelle returned to her desk and began thinking about Alan's question. *You wouldn't design a system with duplicates on purpose, would you?* she thought. *But I guess they could be harmless, or hurting sales less than something else we could fix instead. How could I prove that isn't the case without running an expensive query that requires engineering help?*

Then an idea struck her: The top fifty "whale" products accounted for a huge percentage of marketplace revenue, and because they were so important, Michelle had their sales data right there on her laptop. What if one or more of them suffered from duplication? A quick calculation on a scrap of paper confirmed what Michelle suspected: even with very conservative estimates for duplication rate, consolidating matching records for just a few of the most popular products would produce revenue gains that exceeded the team's entire quarterly target.

She sprinted back to Alan and tossed her figures onto his keyboard. "Look! That's why we need this query," she exclaimed.

Alan read the calculation and looked up at Michelle. "Are you sure this is right?" he asked, surprised. "Why haven't we been working on this already?"

"I don't think anyone thought to check," she replied. "Have I explained the reasoning well enough?"

"I'll say!" said Alan, smiling broadly. "I'll drop my current project and get this query run by the end of the day."

As it turned out, not only did Alan find significant duplication, but he also found a number of quick wins that would address it. Engineers dove in from all directions to code, test, and deploy the changes, with immediate effects on revenue and customer satisfaction. The company now has an entire team devoted to de-duplication work, ensuring that the gains Michelle and Alan envisioned remain in place. And all because Michelle and Alan had been able to find—together—an exciting, motivating Why.

Conclusion: Applying the Why Conversation

In this chapter, you learned how to unstick a conversation by moving from *interests* to *positions*; how to move the conversation forward with transparency and curiosity by *combining advocacy and inquiry*; how to *jointly design* decisions with your team; and how to use the above techniques to identify a motivating Why with your team to which they are internally committed. Unified by a jointly designed Why, you and your colleagues will be able to have productive conflicts instead of interminable debates—a key step in your conversational transformation. You can use the Why Conversation in many ways, including the following:

- An ***executive leader*** can explore technical or product contributions to team purpose and organizational goals that he might not have considered on his own.
- A ***team lead*** can provide effective guidance to her team on topics like which technical shortcuts to take or what features to prioritize, using agreed and well-understood team and company goals to explain her decisions.

- An ***individual contributor*** can bring his experience of testing, deployment, and/or coding to bear on changes to team process or direction, producing better decisions with his and others' internal commitment.

Chapter 6

The Commitment Conversation

For the first time in this book, we're about to talk about how to *execute* better. Using the tools introduced in this chapter will lead to effective, reliable commitments by your team. Execution is typically the first concern we hear about when diagnosing a troubled team: "Our processes are bloated and slow us down." "Users haven't seen improvements for months." "We just don't get much done." So why have we waited so long to address it?

As we'll explain in detail, the reason is that if you haven't first built Trust, reduced Fear, and agreed on Why, execution will only get you to the wrong destination faster. This is exactly the failure mode of the software factory that we discussed in Chapter 1—detailed planning and rigid separation of responsibilities gives the illusion of control and precision, but actual delivery falls far short of the team's potential, because the foundational elements are missing. Executives are puzzled by failure to deliver when the plans seem so precise; team leads scramble to meet impossible deadlines they can't explain to their teams; and individual contributors are terrified into working late, or into the weekend, or for a new employer entirely.

The good news is that by applying the lessons we've covered so far, you're now ready to use the techniques in this chapter to make effective, believable commitments that will be welcomed by an enthusiastic, autonomous team. After adding these methods to your personal conversational toolkit, you'll be able to:

- Identify key words and phrases and *agree on the meaning of these key elements*, ensuring that everyone understands team commitments in the same way.
- Use a *Walking Skeleton* to provide a framework for a series of commitments and show progress toward each.
- Combine these techniques, along with the tools and techniques from previous chapters, to *define and agree on your commitments* while avoiding common pitfalls.

Compliance versus Commitment

"I really liked that we were able to get clear on the scope and research the new tool before we made our commitment," says Bianca, a sysadmin in a team we know, during a retrospective on her team's installation of a new container-management system, which had been completed with minimal downtime. "We knew what we had to do, and we knew how we were going to approach it. That allowed us to commit to the delivery, and the new system is brilliant."

Carlos, a developer in a different team, has no faith in his management's initiative to adopt Agile methods. "They say they want us to change how we work," he says. "But they really only care about hitting deadlines. We'll do this now like they've asked, but in a couple of months there will be some crisis and all this Agile stuff will disappear." Carlos is going along with the plan by attending training on pairing, testing, and estimation, but doesn't really intend to change his day-to-day work habits at all.

We can see from Bianca's comments that she was part of a successful Commitment Conversation—a conversation in which everyone creates and commits to a shared definition of what it means to be "finished" with a project and how to get there—but Carlos is anything but committed. Bianca knew what she was signing up for and was part of the decision to switch container systems, while Carlos's managers simply made decisions and passed down orders to start using Agile methods. Bianca backs her team's new process, while Carlos is just waiting until he doesn't have to follow his anymore.

We hear about "commitment" all the time. Often a team is committing to a deadline, but there are other types of commitment as well. An executive may ask her division to commit to abstract ideals and values, like professionalism or integrity. A regulator may tell a company to commit to very concrete actions, like writing documentation for operational procedures within five working days. We ourselves have frequently asked people if they are willing to "disagree and commit." Why all these requests for commitment?

It is because we want to avoid the alternative: compliance.

Compliance is doing what you are told. At first, this doesn't seem like a bad thing; after all, in many workplaces, compliance is the desired behavior, allowing a stable and effective process to keep running smoothly. However, compliance fails exactly when the process isn't stable, when creativity is needed, when the team needs to identify and overcome unknown obstacles—that is, when you need to create new business value by taking on a new challenge, exactly the situation Agile, Lean, and DevOps software development methods were designed to address.

Compliance without commitment is just going through the motions. From the outside, it might look the same, but people on the team know something is missing. Compliance is showing up; commitment is engaging with your whole self. Compliance is filling the space; commitment is participating. Compliance can be enough for routine day-to-day tasks; compliance is not enough to generate change, to improve, to excel. If these are your aims, you need commitment.

Where does commitment come from? A person may be committed for many personal reasons. Sometimes commitment arises because of a problem someone experiences personally. One developer whom Jeffrey was training on testing said that her motivation was to be able to go home on time on a Friday rather than fix last-minute bugs. For others it is a question of mastery: they believe that a certain skill is part of being a competent professional, and they are therefore driven to have that skill. These idiosyncratic, personal sources of commitment are important, but by their nature, they are hard to plan for or rely upon; it's unlikely that everyone or even most people on your team will come to commitment in these ways. The good news is that there is a highly successful way to seek commitment with every team and with every individual: we can ask for it in the Commitment Conversation, as we'll explain in this chapter.

A successful Commitment Conversation builds upon the other conversations we've described so far:

> If your team has **low Trust**, they'll behave like Carlos, the developer who goes along with the process without really changing anything. Without stories that align with those asking for the commitment,

the Carloses default to cynical beliefs and unproductive actions. "If we work hard to achieve this outcome, they'll just ask us to work even harder next time," they say.

If your team harbors **unmitigated Fear** about the repercussions of missed commitments, then they will be risk averse to a crippling degree, following orders to the letter. After all, if things don't work, it isn't really their fault; somebody else told them to do things that didn't make sense. For people opting for this line of psychological defense, a micromanager is a perfect solution. One person likes giving detailed orders while the other likes being told precisely what to do. The results are generally not very impressive, but it is a comfortable ride—to nowhere.

And if your team was **left out of designing the Why** for the commitment, they won't fully understand it or truly believe in it. Without the chance to put the proposal on the rack, finding all its weakness and edge cases, why should they trust it is a plan that will survive the difficulties ahead and deliver results? "Far safer to just go along with whatever comes down from management and wait for it to fail," they'll say.

But if you have overcome all these obstacles, you are ready for the Commitment Conversation.

Mandy's Commitment Story

I'm Mandy, a product manager in a midsize software company. Our highly skilled Developer Relations team is building a new API (application programming interface—a way for programmers to automate interactions with our service) that the marketing department is very excited to sell. At our last sprint planning session, I tried to get the team to estimate a delivery date to help Marketing, but it blew up in my face. I think I should try to Record one of these conversations and analyze it to help me and my team reach an agreement, and a commitment, on a firm deadline.

Mandy and the Developers' Conversation

Reminder: read the right-hand column first, then go back and read right to left.

What Mandy thought and felt	What Mandy and the developers said
Everyone's waiting for this one—version 1 is really showing its age.	Mandy: Okay! Our next item to estimate is version 2 of the API.
That doesn't sound good.	Zeke: Yeah, right. How long is a piece of string?
I was counting on having this well ahead of the marketing campaign. Is it at risk?	Mandy: Really? I thought we were planning to have it done this sprint.
This doesn't make any sense.	Xavier: That's very unlikely. We just found out that the underlying data won't pass the validations, for a start.
The data has to be good if all our customers are using it.	Mandy: Really? So how is version 1 working then?
I'm not so sure customers really need us to provide completely valid data in the new API. A lot of them already have cleanup scripts.	Walter: It doesn't guarantee validity, but v2 is supposed to.
I thought version 2 was just an overdue tidy-up. Why would it be more complex?	Xavier: There are a lot of complex test cases too. No way we can give you an estimate on those until we try a few.
Maybe I can get some kind of commitment out of them anyway, even if it does take longer than we'd like.	Mandy: So when do you think we can actually have it ready?
There's no way that's acceptable.	Zeke: No way to know. There are just too many uncertainties.
I've got a real problem here. Nobody is going to want to hear this.	Mandy: Really? I don't think that our friends in Marketing are going to like that.

I thought this was going to be a simple estimation, like all the others we do in our pre-sprint meetings, but boy, was I wrong! The team seems really negative about the new version, and I'm really surprised about how hard they think it is to complete. Not having an estimate is going to really mess up the schedule for Marketing. Can't they see that I need them to make a commitment so we can plan?

PREPARING: AGREE ON MEANING

Jeffrey thought he was being very clear. "Will the new login screen be done on Friday?" he asked during the Monday morning planning session. "Absolutely. We estimated it at five days, and there's no reason why it shouldn't be done by then," replied the developers.

On the following Monday, the group reviewed progress from the past week. "I see the new login page isn't working in production," Jeffrey said. "Why wasn't it done on Friday like you expected?"

"But we did finish exactly what we planned to do," came the reply. "The code is live. It works for all our test cases. We've disabled it just for now because the single sign-on integration is playing up and the customer team is looking at it for us. It's done—just not turned on yet." And now we see the classic problem with this commitment: we didn't agree on what it means to be done.

The team had had a very simple form of the Commitment Conversation, but Jeffrey had failed to prepare properly. He knew what he meant when he said "done," and it was all clear in his head. What he didn't do was collect and express his thoughts about exactly what he was looking for from the commitment. He wanted to know, "Will I be able to use this in production on Friday?" What he had actually asked was, "Will this be done?" Jeffrey would have done better to pose the first, more specific question, or alternatively to follow the second with, "And what will customers be able to use after five days?"

Our suggested cure for this type of misunderstanding is to align our language very carefully and explicitly with our conversation partners before and during the Commitment Conversation. As Roger Schwarz says in *Smart Leaders, Smarter Teams: How You and Your Team Get Unstuck to Get Results*, we should "use specific examples and agree on what important words mean."[1] This is helpful in any difficult conversation but particularly when discussing a commitment, because the cost of misunderstanding can be very high:

unless we clarify precisely what we are committing to, any misunderstanding may not be evident until the time of completion, perhaps weeks or even months later, after much wasted effort. That's just what happened to Jeffrey and his team.

Notice that we *didn't* say that in Jeffrey's case the team should agree on a single, public definition of done (DoD), an Agile practice particularly used by Scrum teams. We certainly think that a definition of done can be very helpful, and it might have indeed assisted Jeffrey and his team, but it doesn't give a guarantee against commitment miscommunication. For instance, the team might have defined "done" as "passes all unit tests, product manager verifies functionality, code in production," and by this definition the login screen *was* done. The problem was, as always, an interpersonal one; Jeffrey's thoughts about "done" at the moment he asked differed from those of the developers; and the only way we know to unearth this kind of misalignment is to ask questions like, "What exactly do you mean by 'done'?"*

"Done" is one important word, the meaning of which you'll want to discuss and clarify for the Commitment Conversation, but there are likely to be many others. For instance, it's notoriously hard to capture the target behavior of a complicated software feature like, say, price calculation: "It's $5 per square meter, except for the granite finish which is $6. And members get 10% off. Except on Thursdays, when it's 15%. And . . . " It's very easy to miss one of the special cases or to get lost in the details. Luckily, we have techniques like Gojko Adžić's Specification by Example (SBE),[3] which give us a structured way to have a discussion about real cases of the feature in use and make sure we are fully aligned on how it should work.

And when you're asking for a commitment to a process or cultural change, it's even more important to align on the meaning of your language by using specific examples. Sofar Sounds, a startup that runs house concerts in hundreds of cities around the world, had this difficulty with the meaning of "DIY" (do it yourself). Initially, attendees would put cash in a hat to

---

* There is solid psychological research suggesting that concepts like "done" are not well defined inside our brains. Only through examples can we align about their meaning. For example, try asking ten people whether a clock is furniture or not—you will get a wide variety of answers! See Gregory Murphy's *The Big Book of Concepts* for much more.[2]

support the organization of the event, and musicians weren't paid for their performances—a very informal, DIY experience. When the company moved to fixed-price ticketing and partnered with Airbnb to sell tickets, it tried to communicate with its widely dispersed community about its continued commitment to the DIY spirit, with the additional income allowing Sofar to make some payments to the players and fund further promotion. But this language didn't have the same meaning for many artists, who saw themselves performing for low fees while they imagined large amounts of ticket revenue went to a central, distant home office; it seemed to be less DIY and more "do it for *them*." Only when Sofar shared detailed examples of event income and expenses were they able to overcome the objections. By showing that income was spent largely on local activities like promotion and improved equipment, they demonstrated that the events were still DIY affairs; and with that shared understanding, they were able to regain the commitment of performers to their shows.[4]

So when you are preparing for your Commitment Conversation, consider what words and concepts are liable to be misunderstood, and have explicit, detailed discussions about them with your team. If needed, make a glossary or poster with agreed-upon definitions for key words and phrases. And recheck those definitions at the start of each Commitment Conversation.

Scoring for Agreement: Shared Meaning Fraction

When you want to check how you're doing with agreeing on meaning, score a conversation by circling the most important words in the conversation and verifying that you and your conversation partner have confirmed your common understanding of the definition of each one. The important words will usually include nouns that name key elements of the activity you're discussing ("user," "price," "preference," "subscription") as well as verbs and adjectives that describe how those elements interact ("secure," "valid," "authenticate," "purchase"). Create a fraction showing how many of the words have confirmed, shared meanings (the numerator) over the total number of important words (the denominator):

$$\frac{\textbf{Words with Confirmed and Shared Meanings}}{\textbf{Important Words}}.$$

PREPARING: THE WALKING SKELETON

A promise is a flimsy thing, easily made and just as easily broken. A commitment should be more than a promise—something you make with conviction and knowledge, and execute with creativity and skill. You will be able to make stronger, more confident commitments if you can do two things: keep each commitment as small as possible, and use a framework that makes it easy to deliver your small commitments over and over. The Walking Skeleton technique gives you both of these advantages.

Alistair Cockburn coined the phrase "Walking Skeleton" in the 1990s to describe a repeated pattern he observed in early iterative-delivery teams. As he tells it in *Agile Software Development: The Cooperative Game*, a project designer told him this story:

> We had a large project to do, consisting of systems passing messages around a ring to each other. The other technical lead and I decided that we should, within the first week, connect the systems together so they could pass a single null message around the ring. This way we at least had the ring working.
>
> We then required that at the end of every week, no matter what new messages and message processing was developed during the week, the ring had to be intact, passing all of the previous weeks' messages without failure. This way, we could grow the system in a controlled manner and keep the different teams in sync.[5]

Here, the "ring" that bears the messages is the Walking Skeleton. Like a real skeleton, it gives the system a meaningful structure from which you can discern the final intended form—you can look at a skeleton and immediately distinguish, say, whether it belongs to a fish or a frog, even if you can't tell exactly which species it is. And from just the above description of the ring system, you can determine quickly that it is going to involve some sort of internetwork communication. But unlike a real skeleton, the ring system "walks" because it actually performs a function, passing messages, even if they are initially just trivial ones.

As a result of these two characteristics of the Walking Skeleton, its structure and its function, it also provides a language for describing commitments and a mechanism for their delivery: "By Friday I'll have the payment message passing around the ring, though it may not be validated yet." And it lets the team keep each change very small and immediately deliverable; you can start with a null message, then gradually add content and additional types and routing, until you wind up with the final system.

In modern software design, the Walking Skeleton may manifest as a client-side interface, often in a browser, talking to a very simple back-end system with a database and appropriate integrations to third parties. For instance, London-based startup Unmade helps apparel companies offer customizable clothing using software that integrates with their retail and manufacturing operations. For a recent project, their Walking Skeleton had a stripped-down user interface—little more than a couple of color pickers—and a basic output file sent to the garment manufacturer in a single format, with fixed values for parameters like size and fit. Despite its simplicity, this was enough to produce an actual piece of clothing with user-chosen colors. From this simple interface, Unmade was able to add increasingly more customizations, sizes, and formats every sprint, producing better and better garments, until they delivered the project right on time.

With all of this said, there are two constraints to bear in mind when creating a Walking Skeleton:

1. *Don't leave out any limbs; an incomplete skeleton is worse than useless.* Unmade's system would have been no good as a framework for their commitments if they had entirely left out, say, customization choices or the ability to produce an output file, as they would have been unable to make a real shirt or pair of pants. How could internal and external customers have verified that each delivery along the way was adding value and meeting commitments unless they could look at and put on a physical garment?
2. *Don't confuse a Walking Skeleton with a minimum viable product (MVP).* No one would buy from a shop that carried only one size, so Unmade's first skeletal version of the product was a long way from commercially viable. However, it successfully exercised all the components of the final software system, generating tremendous confidence and providing a delivery mechanism that worked fantastically well to get to the ultimate goal. You may want to produce and use an MVP somewhere along the way as you add features to your skeleton, but your initial skeleton can be much simpler.

What about nonsoftware commitments? The Walking Skeleton is useful here too, with appropriate modifications. A common DevOps pattern is to begin monitoring and publishing information about a system characteristic (say, memory usage) and then use this as a Walking Skeleton, chipping away at the metric with a series of small commitments to reduce the footprint by 5%, then 10%, and so on. Another example: we used a monthly management study group as a Walking Skeleton to help an organization first investigate new ways of managing, then gradually introduced one such change after another, evaluating its progress with each other in the study-group sessions.

Sidebar: The Tilted Slider

The Tilted Slider, shown in Figure 6.1, illustrates the trade-off teams make between perfect predictability and total productivity when making commitments. An example of a highly predictable organization is NASA, which delivers extremely reliable, safety-critical software to a rigid deadline set by the motion of planets and satellites, but whose productivity is glacial compared to most developers—only a few hundred lines of code per developer *per year*.[6]

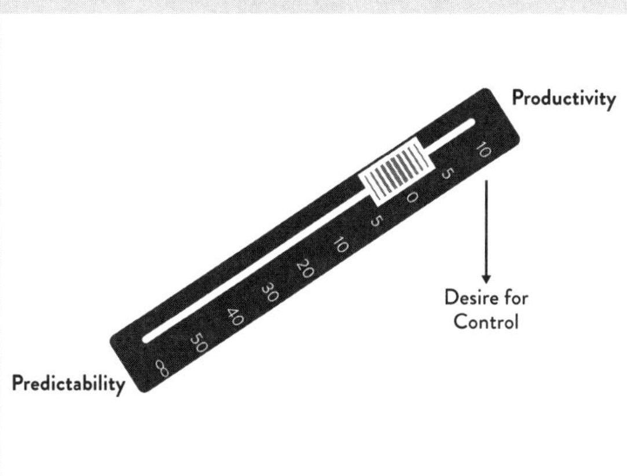

Figure 6.1: The Tilted Slider

By contrast, some pre-launch startups, with tiny development teams, are super productive, as they need almost no process and can shift priorities without fear of annoying their (nonexistent) users. But these startups have never heard of a roadmap or a deadline and are typically absolutely unpredictable in their delivery.

Few teams are at either extreme of the slider, but everyone sits somewhere on the spectrum. Moving the slider toward predictability necessarily means more process, more planning, and less cranking out code. Moving the slider toward productivity means giving up some of the estimation and forward planning that you could be doing in favor of rapid iteration and feedback to correct errors.

The most unusual aspect of this slider is, of course, that it is tilted. This is because there is a force of gravity pulling your team toward the predictable end of the spectrum. This force is the natural human desire for control. A common error is to apply control methods such as formal requirements and change management when, in fact, you could get enough control with methods closer to the productivity end of the slider.

The Tilted Slider can help you with the Commitment Conversation in appropriate circumstances. If your proposed commitment involves delivery of a particular feature or completion of work for a specified deadline, try deciding where your team currently has its Tilted Slider set: closer to the predictable end, to the productive end, or dead in the middle? Discuss this with others in your team to align your views on the current setting. Is this setting effective or would you like to move it? What trade-offs does the current setting imply you are making? What does the current setting mean for your team's velocity? The quality of your output? The predictability of your results? Ideally, you'll have a common view on these questions before you start the Commitment Conversation, so you can adjust your plans to allow for your expected level of productivity or predictability.

The Conversation: Making a Commitment

With the conversational skills you've now built up, the steps to a successful Commitment Conversation are easy—*deceptively easy*—to summarize. First, agree on the meaning of words you'll use in the conversation, perhaps using some TDD for People or Coherence Busting to overcome misunderstandings and fears. Then use your Walking Skeleton to define one or more small steps forward, and agree with your conversation partner on a commitment for those steps. Finally, explicitly confirm the commitment, perhaps by asking everyone involved to restate and accept the commitment, or by posting it publicly on a board or a wiki page.

The three steps to a successful Commitment Conversation are:

1. Agree on the *meaning* of the commitment.
2. Agree on the *next outcome* to commit to.
3. Reaffirm the commitment.

Obstacles to the Commitment Conversation

The steps seem straightforward—but obstacles are waiting to trip you up.

The first obstacle is *cultural*: the idea that voluntary commitment is valuable may be a threatening, unwelcome concept in your environment. Where this is the case, compliance is the order of the day, because managers prefer the illusion that all they need is for their staff to do what they have been asked. After all, they don't have to ask for commitment from machines. And thinking of humans as a kind of machine makes the job of management much simpler, as we pointed out in Chapter 1: you needn't confront the fact that your team doesn't trust you, or that you fear it won't do the job well, or any number of other messy problems that come with those pesky humans.

Management is indeed much simpler if we believe that people doing what they're told is enough. It is easier to staff projects if we consider developers to be interchangeable resources, one of whom can be instantly and painlessly substituted for another. It is even easier if we believe a single engineer can divide her time efficiently among two, three, or even more projects! These beliefs about substitutability and frictionless task-switching fit the Taylorist, person-as-machine model. However, humans aren't like that, and admitting as much might undercut the basis of the management culture, forcing us to confront difficult interpersonal issues that would just be easier to ignore.

If you suspect you have a cultural bias against commitment, or if you encounter resistance that shows this bias does exist, you aren't ready for the Commitment Conversation. Return to earlier chapters to address the issues of Trust, Fear, and Why that underlie this resistance *first*, and then you will find the conversation itself much easier to hold.

The second obstacle, paradoxically, is the *existing commitment process* your team uses, which may be sprint planning, detailed design documents, or simply nodding when the boss gives you a deadline. Whatever method you use, your team may be too comfortable with it—too willing to accept unclear language and overly aggressive deadlines without engaging in a fruitful Commitment Conversation about all your options and about productivity, and inward versus outward investment.

If this describes your experience, try jointly designing your way out of the situation, so your team has participated in designing and holding a Commitment Conversation that works for them. You may also find it helpful to use the Directed Opportunism "briefing" structure that we describe in Chapter 7 to help your team identify what constraints and freedoms they can exercise when helping to shape the commitment.

The final obstacle is *partial acceptance*. No matter what you try, you may find that some members of the group are still stuck in compliance mode and just can't get to a commitment, thanks to indifference, hostility, or simply sheer stubbornness. Luckily, you don't need commitment from everyone! You do need someone or some group who has internal commitment to make a genuine attempt. These people, if they achieve some measure of success, can become champions and evangelists who then engender a committed attempt from others. We've never seen a successful culture or process transformation project, for example, without the unwavering effort of at least a few committed individuals at the start.

When you've overcome these obstacles and have a smooth Commitment Conversation, it will feel great! We remember one of our team meetings a few years ago: We were planning a lengthy project one summer in a hot meeting room. Everyone had argued out all the meanings and defined many small steps on the way to the larger commitment we wanted to make, and we'd added up our estimates on the whiteboard to reach an overall delivery date some five months away. Silence descended, as no one wanted to comment on what was a substantial commitment, until one brave engineer piped up from the back.

"Gee, everyone, there's nothing to be afraid of here. We understand the tasks, and we know each one is individually simple and achievable. If we can't complete this set of tasks by that date, in fact much sooner, we should go into another line of work."

We polled the team, who looked relieved as everyone agreed that the tasks were definitely achievable. Then we emerged into the cool air together, a committed team.

Mandy's Commitment Story Continued

Reflecting and Revising

I'm going to start trying to understand my conversation by reflecting on it and scoring it. I asked two questions, and on reflection, I do think both were genuine—I really did want to know why version 2 was so much more complex than Version 1, and when the feature might actually be ready. On the other hand, my left-hand column shows that I had a lot of doubts about what the developers were saying, and I didn't share them at all. I also notice I said "Really?" a lot when I was surprised or displeased, which seems like a tell.

How about agreeing on meaning? I circled five words or phrases that seem particularly important to the topic: "estimate," "done," "validation," "complex test case," and "ready." Some of my doubts in the left-hand column were about what the developers meant by these words, but I never asked or clarified them specifically. So zero out of five there for me, I think.

To improve and Revise, I'd mainly like to be better at sharing doubts. I can try to notice when we have possible disagreements on meaning and express my concerns right away, instead of suppressing them. That should help me get to a clearer commitment—or at least I hope it will!

Improved Conversation

I sought out David, the tech lead for the Developer Relations team. I wanted to see if we could find a way to work together on creating a commitment that the team and others could both believe in.

Mandy and David's Improved Conversation

What Mandy thought and felt	What Mandy and David said
	Mandy: I was really surprised by the reaction of the team to estimating for the new API.

Yep, I wasn't dreaming. Something is wrong here.

David: Yeah, I got that too. And it's not the first time they've expressed those concerns.

I especially value David's view. Does he think we have a problem?

Mandy: Can you tell me more about the concerns? And what do you think yourself?

How odd. Where did March 4th come from?

David: It's much harder than we thought. And Marketing says it wants it by the 4th of March, no exceptions. The team doesn't see how to finish by then, and frankly, I don't either.

Can David tell me more about this?

Mandy: That's news to me—and an oddly specific date.

Ah, I get it. No one has asked me to get a commitment for early March yet, but I bet a request like that is on the way.

David: I thought so too, until I saw them laying out seating plans. They've rented a hall and invited all our customers for lunch to see the all-new, all-singing, all-dancing API!

I'll remind Dave that features aren't committed until we've agreed to them as a team. I wonder how far off we really are from Marketing's target?

Mandy: Well, the good news is that we haven't actually committed to anything yet, though it sounds like Marketing has. What delivery date might the team accept as reasonable?

Ouch. That's a long time. But I don't understand the meaning of that final phrase.

David: Definitely not before June; July would be better. The data needs a lot of filtering before it's client-ready.

I think "client-ready" isn't needed here, just "good enough to demo."

Mandy: Wait, "client-ready"? What do you mean by that?

Ah, we have the same understanding of the word but a different understanding of the commitment.

David: Well, obviously all the validations have to be in place, and all the tests for edge cases. We can't give bad data to clients.

The distinction is important—I bet he can suggest ways to simplify the scope if we can align on what's needed.	Mandy: I'm not sure we're talking about the same thing. The commitment we need is for something we can demonstrate during a sales pitch, like at this lunch you mentioned, or on a prospect visit. Does that match your understanding?
Yes, now he's got it.	David: I think I see what you're getting at. We just have to be able to show the basic workflow, not the whole working integration.
I need to share the constraint: we have to protect client data from inadvertent disclosure, or the regulator will come down on us hard.	Mandy: Exactly. Does that reduced constraint help at all? We can take reasonable shortcuts, just so long as we don't put real data at risk.
Ah, I really like that, especially the dummy data.	David: Well, we could skip the validations for a start. And we could even use dummy data that we know would be simple to display.
Let's see if we've cleared the commitment obstacle.	Mandy: Both of those scope changes would be fine. Would that help the team to make a confident commitment to March 4th?
That sounds very promising!	David: I'm pretty sure we can find a way to deliver without validations or real data. I'll ask the team this afternoon and let you know by tomorrow morning what I hear.

I wanted to agree on time and scope with David, but we had to clarify several things first: why the team was concerned, when Marketing's target was and why they had picked it, and what the constraints were on the team's work toward the target. Clarifying the meaning of "client-ready" helped us move toward an informed commitment—one that meets the external constraint (deliver by March 4th) as well as an internal one (don't expose customer data). I was really pleased with how this conversation went!

Example Commitment Conversations

Nash and the Sysadmins: Designing the Walking Skeleton

Nash says, "I'm a nontechnical executive in the IT department of a major retailer. We need to set up new sites in seven countries around the world to support a new product line we're launching this quarter. The current estimate from the tech team is six months to launch the new online services, which is way too slow; they tell me the biggest holdup is setting up the servers. I'm visiting a group of three system administrators, Abdul, Becca, and Molly, who work in our development team. My goal is to find out what options we have to get these sites up fast!"

Nash and Sysadmin's Conversation

What Nash thought and felt	What Nash and the Sysadmins said
Let's get the issue on the table. I want to check my information is right first.	Nash: The engineering leads tell me the earliest date we can get the seven new sites up is in February. Is that right?
Okay, confirmed the bad news.	Becca: Yes, that's our best estimate. We're confident about committing to provisioning all the servers then.
It's so annoying that we can't go faster. Surely it's technically possible?	Nash: Argh, how frustrating! The problem is, February is about three months late. We need the sites by November at the latest, for Christmas. What options do we have to meet that target?
I'm glad Molly trusts my motives at least.	Molly: I believe you, and I'd love to say we can do it, but it's just not possible. Even getting backups in place takes many weeks.

That sure sounds inefficient. I wonder why they haven't done anything about this.

Abdul: Not to mention all the manual config. The process is clunky, but we know it works.

Nash: I'm no techie, but those sound like things we could automate. Am I missing something?

I'm assuming there's some way around this. I should verify that I'm right.

Becca: Sure! There are lots of tools that let you stand up servers quickly and repeatably. But IT Risk and InfoSec haven't approved them.

That's what I thought. Why are the internal barriers so high?

Nash: That's true but only for live sites, right? Could we get internal services up faster, and then add patch management, backups and so on later, with the normal approvals?

This might be a way to get a Walking Skeleton going.

Abdul: Sure, but how would that help?

Nash: Well, if the sites are up, the developers can start coding and deploying much sooner, and we can show real progress to Marketing.

A series of small commitments, each met, should build a lot of confidence.

Molly: But that doesn't get us to your deadline. We'll be live internally faster but will still have to jump through all the hoops to make the servers production-ready.

Molly's right, but I may be able to help.

Nash: Let me worry about that. I suspect that showing regular, visible progress will smooth the way for approvals. Using the new tools, can we get bare-bones machines deployed this week, for example?

Abdul: Yes; in fact we can do it in all seven countries.

Better than I thought!

Becca: Agreed. What's more, I'm sure we can whip up a roadmap showing our planned weekly progress for the next two months using the new tools for incremental setup. I'm not sure about anything beyond that, though, and I don't think we'll be done by that point.

Great! Becca gets it too. A plan like this would help me find optimizations elsewhere in tech and get marketing underway too.

Nash: We don't have to be; we can replan as we go, and we'll learn more as we start to use the new setup. Am I right you'd all be comfortable committing to a two-month partial roadmap with weekly deliveries?

I think we're aligned now. Time for a final check on the plan and the commitment.

Well, I didn't get certain delivery by Christmas, but a clearly committed team with a clear plan to execute is a pretty good alternative.

All: Yes!

Nash would have been most happy with an immediate, confident commitment to Christmas delivery of all seven servers. He was pleased, though, that the culture of psychological safety they'd worked to build meant the team could tell him this wasn't realistic. The Walking Skeleton alternative looks promising (as it often does for DevOps challenges), but it may require some intervention from him to get clearance for incremental deployments—a reciprocal commitment Nash makes to the team that he wouldn't have known was necessary without the Commitment Conversation. The Walking Skeleton lets the team work to a set of incremental milestones that are much easier to commit to, and this gives Nash enough to get other teams started. It's a scenario where everybody wins!

Julie and Erik: Committing to a New Process

Julie says, "Recently, I've been finding it really hard to work with Erik, who is the CEO and my boss. He likes participating in decisions like which feature we'll build next or whether to hire another developer, but sometimes it seems to me that getting involved at a low level isn't very efficient for him or healthy for my team. It's hard for me—and others who work with Erik—to tell when he should be informed about or participate in a decision and when he doesn't need to be involved. I've developed a document template that I think might help organize our joint decision-making. It lays out which decisions need Erik's input and which don't, gives space for presenting options, and reminds us to gather data about each option, like its cost and the time it will take to execute. I'm about to talk with Erik about committing to use this new process."

Julie and Erik's Conversation

What Julie thought and felt	What Julie and Erik said
	Julie: Did you have a chance to read the decision document?
This is a good start!	Erik: I did, and I like it! I made a few edits. I'm glad you're working on it.
Let's check our alignment on the basic idea first.	Julie: Super! I'll look at those changes later. More fundamentally, did the idea of a decision process seem valuable to you?
Ouch. That's true, but I think he missed the point.	Erik: Sure. It should help me keep us on track and aligned. I can read all the details and feedback to you on each decision you make.
Deep breath—a little apprehensive about challenging him like this.	Julie: I'm glad you said that, because I'm not sure I agree.
	Erik: Really? What do you mean?
Let me slow down here with a question. Are we agreeing about the underlying assumptions?	Julie: Well, the greatest value in this process for me is that it will help me know whether to involve you in a particular decision at all. Do you agree that it's good for me to make some decisions without you?
A few months ago I wouldn't have trusted this answer, but our stories are better aligned now. I really do think he wants to delegate.	Erik: Yes, of course. As the company grows, I can't do everything; and I have to let other people take the reins sometimes.

This is my key point.	Julie: Okay, we're aligned there for sure. So the part I'm most keen to agree on is how we'll use the decision document in cases where I don't need to involve you.
	Erik: Hmm, I don't follow. In that case, why would you need to fill it in?
	Julie: Well, this section at the top describes when to use the document. If a decision doesn't meet these criteria, we stop and don't use the document at all.
I'm glad I probed and clarified. Now I'm much more confident that we're aligned.	Erik: Aha, because it's low enough level that I don't need to be involved. I didn't quite follow that section, but I get it now.
Final check—are we committing now?	Julie: So you're okay if I, and others, use those criteria as a filter?
Sounds like a commitment to me!	Erik: Sure, though some of them need a little tweaking. The budget limit can be higher, for example. But I'm definitely keen to start using this now.

Notice how Trust entered at a crucial moment here. Given Erik's history of micromanagement, Julie could have easily discounted his assertion that he wanted her to make some decisions independently, but having gone through a Fear Conversation, where Erik's time was identified as a possible limiting factor in company growth, she chose to believe her aligned story that he really did. This is the building of a Commitment Conversation on the foundation of earlier conversations. Agreeing on meaning was very important as well—the two of them could easily have "agreed" to the process without Erik fully understanding that it included delegation criteria, meaning that he was committing to *not* doing some things. This would surely have led to a lot of confusion and frustration. We're pleased to report that Erik and Julie adopted and still use the decision framework, with great results!

CASE STUDY: CONTEXT FOR COMMITMENT

Doing What They're Told

Anna Shipman, technical director of customer products at the *Financial Times*, had a compliance problem, as she outlined in her blog.[7] There was nothing obviously wrong. Seven months into her role as technical director, her team of fifty-five engineers was successfully running the newspaper's main website, as well as satellite brands, and Android and iOS apps. With almost a million paying users around the world,[8] the site had to remain constantly up to date with the latest news, load instantly on all devices, and add new features daily. With both continuous deployment and A/B testing running on overdrive, the team was delivering improvements hundreds of times a week, experimenting nonstop, and keeping up with internal and external customer demand.

But Anna knew there was still something holding back the team. She could sense it in her own day-to-day work as she handed out assignments to her five principal engineers. Whether she did this in their weekly meeting, over Slack or email, or in person, a nagging feeling told her something wasn't right. "I was still in control of the flow of tasks," she said. "I felt there must be a better way to do this so that the principals know the problems . . . that I need help with (and also know about the problems I don't know about)."[9] In short, she wanted commitment, not mere compliance.

Like many managers, Anna was finding that when you tell your staff what to do, they do it—and that was the opposite of the creative, innovative team that their Agile practices could support. Instead, her goal was for her management team to be self-organizing and autonomous, so that "each of them [would] be a good candidate to take over [her] job."[10] And that couldn't happen while she was stuck in the role of chief task distributor.

Tearing Out the Filter

After seeking advice from colleagues and from peers about how to give more autonomy to her principal engineers, Anna resolved to have what we'd call a Commitment Conversation with them. Her goal was to jointly design a better way of interacting—one that would let them commit to tasks themselves, without undue dependence on her.

She started by explaining that she'd been filtering out contextual information from the rest of the business, such as incoming feature requests, status reports from other teams, and financial results. She said she "didn't want to drown [the] team in emails,"[11] so she'd protected them from this tsunami of outside input. For her, the emails and requests were distractions that she needed to shield her team from.

But the principal engineers responded in a surprising way: they asked to receive more unfiltered information, not less. This would allow them to make sensible prioritization and optimization decisions. Further, if someone brought up an issue, they would be familiar with it rather than baffled or confused; they would be able to make informed commitments and deliver on them. The meaning of the outside input was very different to them: it was valuable context.

"Essentially I thought I was protecting them and helping them do their jobs," said Anna later, "but in fact I was actually blocking the information flow and making it harder for them to do their jobs."[12]

Once they'd agreed on a common meaning for the incoming contextual information through a Commitment Conversation, Anna and her principal engineers committed to take several steps to share context among themselves:

- They set up a mailing list and asked others to use it for requests rather than just emailing Anna. She also forwarded emails to this list that she thought the group might find helpful. This formed the Walking Skeleton that would allow the group to take on the other initiatives.
- Anna brought one or more of the principal engineers to relevant meetings and sometimes even sent them in her place. Attendees shared meeting notes with the rest of the group on the mailing list afterward.
- The group extended their weekly meetings and used a color-coded kanban board to track tasks and share information about them.
- Anna spent more time on her team's Why, sharing the results of her thinking on the mailing list, an internal wiki, and an external conference talk.[13]

"Solved before I've Heard about It"

The results from the commitment to share more context were dramatic. The group email address became the destination for most requests, allowing all of its members access to more information so they could react accordingly. The principal engineers were able to pass work to each other's teams when they were overloaded, increasing the odds of a successful delivery. And "quite often," Anna says, "someone will email or mention . . . a problem that they have picked up and solved before I've even heard that it exists."[14] They had found and used untapped potential in the development organization—and it's all thanks to the Commitment Conversation.

Conclusion: Applying the Commitment Conversation

In this chapter, you learned to *identify key concepts and clarify their meaning*, to *use a Walking Skeleton* to provide structure to your commitments, and to *make commitments effectively* using these techniques and those from previous chapters. The productive Model II reasoning promoted by your conversational transformation creates the right environment for effective commitments, while delivery on those commitments promotes Trust and reduces Fear to move the transformation forward still further. You can use the Commitment Conversation in many ways, including the following:

- An ***executive leader*** can align the work culture among multiple departments, like Engineering and Sales, by expecting believable, easily tracked commitments from each, and tracking progress on those commitments.
- A ***team lead*** and her team can make commitments such as sprint goals and build-measure-learn targets with confidence and enthusiasm.
- An ***individual contributor*** can participate in defining commitments and contribute to their fulfillment.

Chapter 7

The Accountability Conversation

Within the feature factory, it would be unimaginable to be completely transparent about delivery and its challenges—why bother, when we're stifled by rigid dicta at every turn? And the same lack of autonomy makes it pointless to be curious about options for varying goals and tactics, since no variation would be achievable anyway. But as we've built Trust, removed Fear, defined Why, and honored Commitment, we've become much more autonomous and unconstrained; and this level of transparency and curiosity is now possible with our final conversation: Accountability.

Executives will find that accountability leads their departments to learn about and correct errors like prioritizing the wrong feature or overspending on cloud servers much earlier and much more efficiently. Team leads will use the Accountability Conversation to clarify sprint and team goals, discover options for achieving those goals, and radiate their team's intentions for feature builds and architectural changes. And individual contributors will no longer say, "We're stuck supporting old browsers" or "Some idiot told us to skip the tests." They will know what the constraints and freedoms are for their work, and where they can exercise creativity in meeting targets.

After absorbing the ideas in this chapter, you will be able to:

- Use *Theory Y* to create a culture that fosters healthy accountability.

- Give *briefings and back briefings* that let the team efficiently and accurately render an account of its actions.
- Use the Accountability Conversation to *radiate intent*, so that everyone concerned with your work can provide help, advice, or corrections in an efficient and supportive way.

Who's Accountable?

"Not another one!" exclaimed Danny. "That's the second feature this week that's been delayed. At this rate, we won't have anything at all to demonstrate on Friday."

As the CTO of a rapidly growing startup, Danny has more teams working for him than ever before. Back when the company was smaller, he was able to divide his time among all the engineers and know exactly how each was doing. But these days, there just isn't time to talk with every team member during every sprint; and he's losing touch with day-to-day progress.

The email he'd just read was typical: the mobile developers were behind again, and one of their app changes wouldn't be ready by the end of the sprint. They weren't alone; nearly every week, at least one team had bad news for him, and often two or three would report slippages.

Danny knew all too well that development doesn't always go to plan. And in fact, he enjoyed the part of his job where developers came to him with problems—he loved discussing technical options and working with product designers and the business to find creative solutions. With many of the older teams, this dynamic was still working well, and the developers did come to him with problems; there were minor snags and bugs, to be sure, but he didn't fear a nasty surprise at the end of a sprint. However, some of the newer teams were much more unpredictable, with major features slipping by weeks and sometimes months.

Danny put his head in his hands and tried to come up with a plan. Should he introduce a daily progress report? Hire a delivery manager? Replace one of the team leads? He wasn't sure what step to take next, but he knew something had to change.

Danny's response is a common one. If we are being repeatedly, unpleasantly surprised—missed deadlines, system downtime, budget shortfalls—we want to take action to end those surprises. The normal approach is to ask for more detailed information, to provide more specific instructions, or to put in more detailed controls. Or sometimes all three! Unfortunately, these instinctive responses often make things worse, because they miss the root of the problem: accountability.

What do we mean by being accountable? We mean simply being obligated to render an account of what you have done and why. A feeling of accountability, held by each person, is one of the keys to success. Accountability is akin to ownership, to responsibility, and to agency. If I am in control of how I spend my time, then only I am able to provide the information on why I have done what I've done, providing the reasoning and the intent behind my actions.

Notice that we are defining accountability very differently from most people. When we hear a manager saying she will "hold someone accountable," our instinct may be to duck under the nearest desk; the phrase connotes correction or punishment for doing something wrong. (See the sidebar on the next page for a historical perspective that may explain this fear.) The person being held accountable is expected to feel contrite, to learn from their mistakes. By contrast, our definition suggests that you can be accountable for a success, a failure, or a neutral result. But "Let's hold someone accountable for doubling sales last month!" is probably not a sentence any of us hear very often.

Our version of accountability—the obligation to explain our results—is key to the self-organization that Agile, Lean, and DevOps teams aim for. Each team member is empowered to make their own decisions about how to allocate time and energy. However, with this empowerment comes an expectation to share what those decisions are and why they were made. Sometimes the Accountability Conversation takes the form of sharing intentions: "Here is what I'm planning to do and why." Other times it is a debriefing or a formal report on a past event. Whatever form this accountability takes, Danny will be able to scale his efforts more successfully if he suppresses his instinct for control and, instead, builds a culture of accountability within his team.

This probably sounds simple to do; and yet being effectively accountable is a learned skill. It requires, as usual, difficult emotional work, cultural change, and much practice. In particular, an effective Accountability Conversation requires high Trust ("I believe you will share my story about how I performed"), low Fear ("I know you won't overreact to my account of what I did"), an agreed Why ("We are headed for this vision, and here's how far we got today"), and a clear Commitment ("Here's my account: I committed to do A and what actually happened was B"). You're more likely to succeed if you and your team have had each of these conversations before embarking on the Accountability Conversation.

Sidebar: Medieval Accountability

Why does the word "accountable" typically have a punitive connotation? We think it might have to do with the origins of the word. "Accountable" literally means "rendering an account," with "account," in turn, coming from the Old French for "reckon" or "enumerate."[1] The word first entered English in medieval times, when it was used to describe the actions of twelfth-century sheriffs. These sheriffs or "shire-reeves," unlike their gun-slinging Wild West descendants, were essentially revenue collectors for the far-flung Angevin Empire. Each was given a "farm," an amount to be paid to the king every year, and was free to extract that amount from his territory more or less as he pleased. Many sheriffs profited handsomely by demanding much more than their assigned farm from their over-awed citizens, keeping the excess for themselves.[2]

The administration of Henry II (King of England, 1154–1189) decreed that the sheriffs would be summoned to his court every Michaelmas (the 29th of September), where they were to bring the annual receipts—in cash, of course (no checks or credit cards in the 1100s!)—to be counted and handed in.[3] Arithmetic was an uncommon skill, so the treasurer and his assistants used the Exchequer, a sort of chessboard, along with a set of counters to represent and compute the money owed to the Crown by the sheriff, and any setoffs from that amount.[4] The exchequer board came to represent the whole process, which became known as "the Exchequer" of a particular year.[5] Each sheriff came forward in turn to describe that year's income and to remind the treasurer about any exceptions or deductions. When an agreed total was computed, the sheriff would hand over a bag of silver pennies to settle his debt.[6] A sheriff who was found to be short of the correct amount could be fined or imprisoned on the spot.[7] So if you think reporting a missed sprint goal is worrying, imagine what a fraught experience it was to be accountable in the twelfth century!

Nicole's Accountability Story

I'm Nicole, a product director with responsibility for multiple teams in our organization. Bobby is the product manager for one of these teams. He frequently seems to misunderstand what I'm asking him to work on, meaning that we often have to stop halfway through a feature or project, reset expectations with the developers, and change half the code. It's getting bad enough that I'm considering firing Bobby, but I've started to wonder whether my own management style and communication approach might be contributing to the problem. Starting with the first R (Record), I've documented our last interaction to see whether I can find ways to improve.

Nicole and Bobby's Conversation

Reminder: read the right-hand column first, then go back and read right to left.

What Nicole thought and felt	What Nicole and Bobby actually said
I hope this makes sense to you.	Nicole: Here's the mockup of the new cash-flow report.
Good question!	Bobby: Okay. How is it different from the one we have today?
	Nicole: Well, for one thing, it's to be updated daily. And it's broken down according to our new global regions, instead of being aggregated.
	Bobby: Got it.
Is that all you need to know? I guess the mockup is fairly self-explanatory.	Nicole: When do you think you can have it ready?
Wow, that's quick! Finance will be really pleased. I just hope you won't miss anything like last time.	Bobby: I'll have to check with the team, but I expect we can finish it in the next sprint.
	Nicole: That would be great!

I felt pretty good about this conversation at the time; however, when the team demonstrated the new report a week later, I was a lot less happy. The team had used comma-separated values instead of Excel format, hadn't included Australia as a region, and made a bunch of smaller errors. Why can't Bobby get these things right?

PREPARING: THEORY X AND THEORY Y

The Motivation Dichotomy

Is it reasonable to expect accountability from your team? Are employees self-interested, moved to action only by direction from above, and incapable of explaining their actions? Or are they interested in success, motivated by a desire to do well, and responsible for their behavior? Management theorist Douglas McGregor, in *The Human Side of Enterprise*, called these two views of employee motivation Theory X and Theory Y (see Table 7.1).[8]

Theory X is closely related to the Taylorist view explored in Chapter 1. It says that workers are lazy and dumb, and must be presided over by managers. When they screw up, they need to be sent to the naughty corner to learn from their mistakes. "I'm not getting results from my workers? The solution is more management," says the Theory X manager. "If I'm not getting the insight into progress that I expect, and if I'm not hearing about issues in time to fix them, then I'll hire a manager to get that information." Accountability for individual contributors is nonsensical if you subscribe to Theory X. The workers have no investment in their own actions nor do they have meaningful involvement in the planning, so it is silly to ask them to explain those actions or the consequences. Instead, you should ask the relevant manager—it is their job to know.

Theory Y is a fundamentally different view of humanity. It says that people want to be engaged, that they want to take ownership, and that they carry the drive for success within themselves. If we believe Theory Y, then the Theory X model of management is not just harmful, it's wasteful. We get better results more cheaply by using the drive for success inherent in each individual. And in a Theory Y organization, accountability is vital. Our motivated, responsible workers need and want to tell managers and collaborators alike about their activities and results; and they also thirst for accurate feedback on those results, to adjust their actions appropriately.

Looking back at the Agile, Lean, and DevOps principles from Chapter 1, we can see a strong bias toward Theory Y:

- Give motivated individuals the environment and the support they need, and trust them to get the job done.
- Empower the team.
- Trust that everyone is doing their best for the business.

THEORY X	THEORY Y
Attitude	
People dislike work, find it boring, and will avoid it if they can.	People need to work and want to take an interest in it. Under the right conditions, they enjoy it.
Direction	
People must be forced or bribed to make the right effort.	People will direct themselves toward a target that they accept.
Responsibility	
People would rather be directed than accept responsibility (which they avoid).	People will seek and accept responsibility, under the right conditions.
Motivation	
People are motivated mainly by money and fears about their job security.	Under the right conditions, people are motivated by the desire to realize their own potential.
Creativity	
Most people have little creativity—except when it comes to getting around rules.	Creativity and ingenuity are widely distributed and grossly underused.

Niels Pflaeging, "Why We Cannot Learn a Damn Thing from Toyota, or Semco."

Table 7.1: Theory X and Theory Y

This is no surprise, of course; as we've looked at each of the previous four conversations, we've seen story after story of software teams succeeding through behaviors consistent with Theory Y, like building trust, explaining motivation rather than imposing a vision, and providing context to drive commitment. In fact, we agree with Niels Pflaeging that adoption of Theory Y is a *precondition* for success with Agile, Lean, or DevOps methods.[9]

Drama or Leadership?

So what puzzles us is why Theory X is still so pervasive in teams that are, at least in theory, adopting people-centric software methods. Why would anyone retain a cultural schema that actively discourages accountability (in our sense)?

We'll leave an exhaustive answer to the social scientists, but we suspect a contributing factor may be the examples shown in television and movies, which supply our first models of leadership. Some films portray the strong, decisive leader barking orders—someone who is firm but fair. Tough. Not afraid of calling out someone who is screwing up. The other trope is the ineffective manager, *Dilbert's* "pointy-haired boss," who is always asking for status reports and nitpicking the details while missing the big picture. Neither of these approaches are examples of effective leadership, in part because they are at odds with true accountability (the decisive leader won't listen to the account, and the indecisive one can't make up their mind about what to do with the information). Both styles lead to unproductive conflict in the organization—but conflict is exactly what creates drama, which is what sells movie tickets and Netflix subscriptions, thus accounting for the popularity of these approaches in films and television.

In contrast, media models of interdependence and self-organization are much more limited. The only prominent dramatic portrayal of a Theory Y leader we can think of is Patrick Stewart's Captain Picard in the *Star Trek* franchise, who regularly gathers all views from his crew members before reacting to a new observation or event, and then frequently delegates the bold, dangerous intervention to others. Superhero groups like The Avengers, or the protagonists of the occasional ensemble movie like *Stand By Me*, portray interdependent groups of people with very different skills who overcome obstacles by using whatever strengths each can contribute; they are also accountable to each other for their decisions and their consequences. But these are exceptions that seem far from daily life.

What can you do to overcome this bias toward Theory X? As with most changes like this, we recommend that you enlist sympathetic team members to help you identify and overcome Theory X beliefs and habits in your organization. For instance, you might renew your commitment to psychological safety (see Chapter 4), share business context as Anna Shipman and her team did (see Chapter 6), and celebrate those who take on additional responsibilities. Simply by holding the Accountability Conversation, you will be sending a powerful cultural message about autonomy and internal motivation.

PREPARING: DIRECTED OPPORTUNISM

Marching Away from Naïveté

Another obstacle standing in the way of the Accountability Conversation is naïve realism.[10] This is the view that we see the world objectively and without bias, and further, that other people will come to the same conclusions as we do, based on the same observations. When we adopt this simplistic view of the world, we see less need to communicate and certainly see no requirement to render an account; after all, everyone else observes the same things we do, so why would we need to explain our actions or their results? Of course, this approach is misguided, and we need the Accountability Conversation precisely because others may have information we don't possess; and they may draw different conclusions about results than we do.

There is a structured way to eliminate our bias toward naïve realism, and from a surprising source: the practices of the Prussian military in the nineteenth century. Stephen Bungay describes this method, which he calls "Directed Opportunism," in his book *The Art of Action: How Leaders Close the Gaps between Plans, Actions and Results*.[11]

Bungay begins with a description of "friction," the sum of all those ways Murphy's Law ("whatever can go wrong *will* go wrong") does its work. The results of friction are three gaps that arise in our attempt to convert the outcomes we desire into plans, our plans into actions, and those actions into the outcomes we intended (see Figure 7.2 on page 164):

- The *knowledge gap* is the difference between what we would like to know and what we actually know.
- The *alignment gap* is the difference between what we want people to do and what they actually do.
- The *effects gap* is the difference between what we expect our actions to achieve and what they actually achieve.

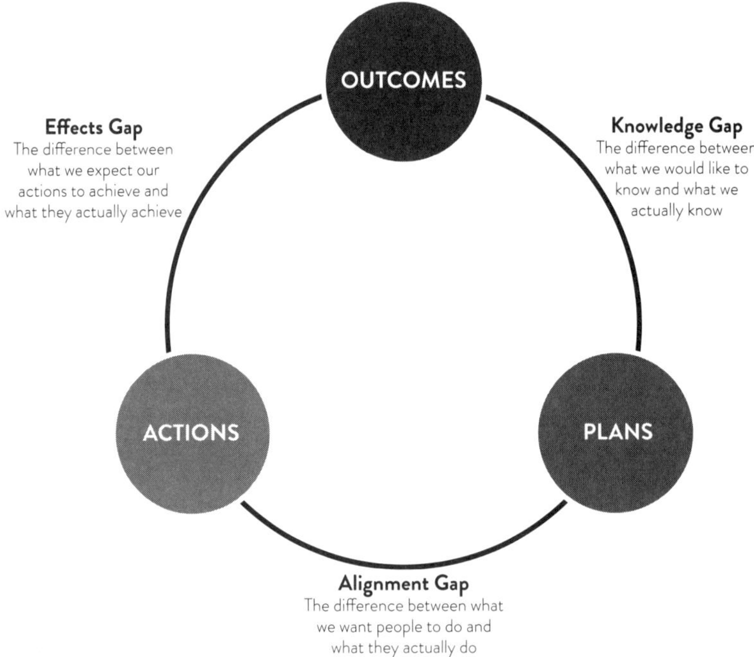

Figure 7.2: Bungay's Three Gaps

Adapted from "Executing Strategy: Some Propositions," StephenBungay.com, accessed October 3, 2019, https://www.stephenbungay.com/ExecutingStrategy.

The management-centric approach to the three gaps above is to try and eliminate them. To close the knowledge gap, leaders seek more detailed information. To close the alignment gap, they give more specific instructions. And to close the effects gap, they implement more detailed controls. Fully closing the gaps is impossible, however, and our increasingly determined attempts to do so cause suffering. In response to such authoritarian micromanagement, "commitment is replaced by compliance, energy is sapped, and morale declines."[12]

As an alternative, Bungay offers his Directed Opportunism method, which he reverse engineered from the strategic and tactical innovations of Prussian military leaders during their wars with France, Denmark, and Austria during the 1800s. The Prussians found that communicating plans and intentions clearly, both up and down the chain of command, was vital for mastering the increasing complexity of nineteenth-century warfare. Thus the core of Directed Opportunism is a protocol between the parties: one person uses a briefing to describe *where we are going*, and the other uses a "back briefing" to explain *how we plan to get there.*

Aligning through a Briefing

In a briefing, one person communicates her intended outcome, provides constraints within which that outcome should be sought, and describes freedoms available during execution. For example, Bungay tells the story of a commander who told two of his generals to move their divisions north to surround the French (outcome) without being slowed down by engagement with the enemy (constraint), and by using whatever route made the most sense for them (freedom).[13]*

By providing the desired outcome and its associated freedoms and constraints, the person providing the outcome is being accountable. They are providing information only they can provide, such as priorities and the trade-offs they value. This is very different from the Theory X approach, with plans handed down from on high, where what the organization wants to achieve is, at best, intermixed with how things should be done; and there is little to no freedom to stray from the dictated path.

Besides being wasteful of human resourcefulness, this approach of planning from the top often falls into the knowledge gap, where the managers doing the planning lack the knowledge and experience of those closer to where the work is done. How could the Prussian commander possibly know the right route for his subordinates to choose from miles away, and without the benefit of modern battlefield information sources, like drones and radios? Far better to equip them with clear intent and allow them to make the right choice based on the local data that only they have.

A good example of a clear briefing was provided by Boeing during the design phase of their 777 airliner.[14] Designers were struggling with lowering the overall weight of the airplane while also keeping the cost within the planned budget. How could they get the best trade-offs between weight savings

* Unlike the military, in a business situation, the relation of the parties may not be leader and follower; a product manager could brief the marketing team on how to coordinate an upcoming feature launch, for example.

and cost savings in the design for the whole craft? Should they, for example, use a more expensive rudder to save weight while changing to more efficient but heavier landing gear? With hundreds of engineers working in separate groups on a large number of subsystems, it was very difficult to see where it was even possible to make such a swap of cost for weight on widely separated, unrelated parts of the airplane.

The solution Boeing found was to provide a briefing to engineers about what trade-offs they could and should make on their local subsystem in the form of simple cost guidelines. An engineer could spend up to $300 to save a pound without approval; spending up to $600 per pound needed only a local supervisor's okay; and even more, up to $2,500, could be spent to save a pound if a program manager gave the go-ahead. These guidelines clarified the constraints within which the engineers needed to work, providing a framework that allowed them to make decisions while ensuring that those decisions were aligned with the overall goal of minimizing cost and weight.

Cementing Agreement with a Back Briefing

If we stopped the Directed Opportunism protocol with just a clear briefing, we would already have a great improvement, with at least one party providing accountability. However, even with a detailed briefing, it is easy for misunderstandings, both large and small, to arise. To account for and detect these imperfections, we also schedule a response to the briefing: a "back briefing" led by the executing party, which is meant to describe how it plans to achieve the desired outcome and to confirm that this plan matches the original outcome, constraints, and freedoms. This accounting for what people plan to do and why they plan to do it—this sharing of reasoning and intent—ensures that there is alignment across all parties.

In *The Art of Action*, Bungay shows us the letter written by von Moltke, the chief of the Prussian General Staff, the commander mentioned earlier, who wanted two of his armies to pursue and surround the French. His letter describes the situation, his intention, the role of each general, and special directions in case the French crossed into Belgium. The letter finishes by providing a deadline for the generals to inform him of the instructions they would be issuing to their armies.[15] The generals' responses were back briefings, which allowed von Moltke to coordinate the movement of his own army with that of his subordinates, and to correct any misinterpretations.

With one of our own clients, a children's retailer, we set up a system of back briefings in which the COO would review product plans with the leadership of each team. Before one of these sessions, we could see how excited the product manager was to share the plans for the revised e-commerce shop through which parents would be able to purchase from a widely expanded range of products. During the meeting, however, the COO looked less and less pleased as the product manager showed screenshots and early prototypes of the new pages. Eventually he said, "But where do we explain the benefits?" It turned out that in focusing on supporting new product types and exciting new ways to buy them, the team had forgotten that the site had to sell the products as fun and educational, something the marketing group was relying on it to do. It was painful to revise the plans but much better to have caught the problem early, before much code had been written. Clearly, the combination of briefing and back briefing is a powerful method for creating mutual accountability.

Scoring for Briefings and Back Briefings

You can score a conversation as a briefing if it involves *making a request*. Display your score as a fraction over three, providing yourself one point for each of the three elements: intended outcome, constraints within which that outcome should be sought, and freedoms available during execution. If you provided *some* constraints or *some* freedoms but not all, give yourself partial credit, such as 0.5 if you described half the constraints. For example, if you shared your intended outcome and all the constraints but did not describe any freedoms, you score would be $\frac{2}{3}$.

Similarly, you can score a conversation as a back briefing if you are *responding to a request*. As with the briefing, display your score as a fraction over three and give yourself one point for including each of three elements: your intended action, your reasoning for adopting that action, and your confirmation that your plans match the briefing provided by the other person.

The Conversation: Radiating Intent

Say you're planning to drive to a holiday destination with your family. How do you decide who needs what information and when to share it? Collaborating on a road trip is very similar to interacting with your team using the Accountability Conversation.

The start of the journey is straightforward, but before we embark, we need to have a shared understanding of the information required for planning—the briefing. This includes the intended outcome ("We're going to the lake house via Sacramento, where we're picking up your sister") as well as the constraints ("Avoid highway 5; too much traffic") and available freedoms ("We can stop at your favorite restaurant"). Once this is clear, we should then return with the equivalent of the back briefing: the intended route, the reasoning for proposing that route, and a request for confirmation that the intended route seems satisfactory. But what happens once the trip starts?

A car driving down even the straightest of roads requires many imperceptible nudges to stay aligned with the white lines, and surprises like a vehicle stopping suddenly or a child running into the road require immediate adjustment.* Passengers don't expect the driver to keep them informed of these constant course corrections, and similarly don't expect the driver to ask permission to respond to an emergency. However, if the driver hits the brakes suddenly, giving the rest of the riders a jolt, the passengers do expect an explanation! They would also expect some communication if there was new information that changed the route or the constraints ("It's raining at the lake; let's head for the mountains instead"), whether it's the driver or the kids in the back who have the new information. Everyone involved with the project has an obligation to contribute to their part of the Accountability Conversation.

What about communication with people who aren't in the car?

Signaling for Success

Technologist Elizabeth Ayer suggests that just as drivers display continuous directional signals before and during a turn, you should be "radiating intent" at all times.[16] We think this is great advice that can yield unexpected benefits: when we are transparent with our intentions, we allow other people to provide relevant information, adjust their plans, and even help us achieve our aims. Radiating intent indiscriminately allows us to get these benefits at times we

* These statements are as true of a self-driving car as of a human-piloted one; somebody needs to be steering and making moment-to-moment adjustments, whether the driver is carbon- or silicon-based.

might not have anticipated; signaling for a turn might help you the most when you (incorrectly!) think there's no one there to see it.

When deciding what information you'd like to radiate, keep in mind these key elements:

- *Share the current state*: "We are trying to select a crash-reporting tool for our mobile apps with a cost that lies within our budget. We've spoken to two companies so far, neither of whom have products that meet our standards."
- *Describe plans and intended outcomes*: "We are seeing three more vendors next week, and also exploring an in-house solution. We should have a workable solution by the end of the month."
- *Alert to obstacles*: "It's possible that the budget reforecast will mean we have to drop this project entirely. We'll know by Thursday."

With an appropriate Theory Y mind-set, and by using the mutual learning tools you've been practicing in previous chapters, you should find that the Accountability Conversation is informative and valuable for keeping your project on track. But be wary—the Accountability Conversation is not a once-and-done affair.

Trusting and Verifying

"He trusts, but he doesn't verify," said the head of Engineering at one of our clients, describing the CEO. (The familiar phase "Trust but verify" was Ronald Reagan's famous dictum, derived from a Russian proverb, about negotiating nuclear treaties with the Soviet Union.[17]) "He gave us the vision and the focus for our team," she continued, "but without regular interaction, we weren't able to stay aligned. We pursued a version of the mission that was flawed; and when he flew in from headquarters to see us, he said we had to scrap three months of work and start over."

We find that one of the most difficult things about the Accountability Conversation isn't having the discussion itself but remembering to *continue* having it. Like our client's CEO, you may think that you're done once you've agreed on the direction for a project—especially if you've used a briefing and a back briefing to double-check for alignment on the desired outcome, the freedoms, and the constraints. After all, won't the other party resent our intrusion? Doesn't

Theory Y say we should trust others' good intentions and leave them alone to get on with the task?

These are valid objections, as micromanagement is to be avoided whenever possible (we don't want someone in the back seat telling us how to steer the car); but neither party to the Accountability Conversation should be disengaging lest disastrous misalignment strikes. The briefer needs to hear how execution is progressing, because they have an obligation to check alignment and the responsibility to coordinate their own actions. In addition, the briefed party needs feedback on their progress as well as updates on how the external situation is changing, especially if that affects the work to be done. The frequency of check-ins will vary with the importance of the project and its level of risk, but "set it and forget it" is not the philosophy we suggest when it comes to the Accountability Conversation.

Using Agile Radiators

Luckily, modern software development methods come with ceremonies and processes that are perfect for triggering the initial Accountability Conversation and providing regular opportunities to radiate intent and progress.

> *Planning*. Scrum, XP, and similar methodologies give us a natural time for discussing accountability: the sprint planning session. Lean or Kanban teams have more frequent, pull-triggered planning activities but still need to break down tasks and agree on acceptance criteria, often during or just after the daily standup. During your team's planning activity, ensure you include time to discuss all three elements of the Accountability Conversation: current state, intended outcomes, and potential obstacles. Going beyond the usual roadmapping and estimation activities to include more context will often prompt ideas and help from other members of the team. Publishing the results of your planning session in an email or company chat, for example, also encourages broader discussion and further opportunities to be accountable to those not directly involved in your work.

> *Information radiators*.[18] A common DevOps practice is to display system metrics—site visitors, memory used, response time—on big monitors in the team area. Agile and Lean teams often have burndown charts

and kanban boards that are displayed electronically, or maintained on a whiteboard or easel. One of our clients maintains a board that shows all their prospective clients and their current stage in the commercial pipeline, to keep the technology team informed about likely incoming sales requests.* In all these cases, the visible indicator is a perfect prompt for an Accountability Conversation based on the information on display. Those inside the team can invite others to visit their radiators for this discussion, or people outside the team can walk by and begin a conversation based on what's displayed.

Retrospectives. An end-of-sprint or end-of-project reflection on recent progress is a natural time to be curious about how ongoing projects are progressing, especially when looking for obstacles that can be removed. Avoid turning the retrospective into a status report, which is not its purpose; instead, remember Theory Y by ensuring that the team is collectively driving the conversation, reflecting on its current condition, its plans, and what can be done to increase the chances of success.

Demonstrations. One of our favorite ways to radiate intent is to demonstrate working software. This can be at the end of a sprint, at the time of delivery to a client, or even better, just when the feature is done. Try to avoid "demonstrating" user-invisible changes like database updates; instead, focus on structure work, so the current and future states are obvious to nontechnical observers (the Walking Skeleton in Chapter 6 can be a big help). If possible, record video of the demonstration and publish it widely, to radiate information to those who are remote or can't attend the demo.

A successful Accountability Conversation should feel positive for all involved, even if there are surprising results or significant obstacles to report. At the end of such a conversation, you will have shared the current state of the project, made next steps clear and discussable, and identified obstacles. Each of these should give all parties the

* You can check out an example here: https://www.leadingagile.com/2017/11/information-radiators-information-vaults/.

opportunity to clarify and revise the intended outcome, freedoms, and constraints for the work to be done. In our experience, teams that do this successfully build the right software and are happy with their destination, even if it wasn't what they imagined at the start.

Nicole's Accountability Story Continued

Reflecting and Revising

Okay, let's try scoring the conversation, even though it sounded just fine to me at the time; maybe I'll Reflect and find something to Revise. I notice I didn't ask any questions at all, so that's a zero over zero straight off. I had some doubts about Bobby's understanding in my left-hand column, but I didn't share them, hoping that he would figure out what I meant. And a twitch I notice is that I tend to default to accepting a confident "got it" when, in fact, it might be wiser to ask more questions.

Scoring the briefing, I don't think I included any of the elements fully. Being really charitable, maybe my explanation of the differences from the current report communicated half of the desired outcome. But I definitely didn't mention freedoms (the developers would have been welcome to order the columns in any convenient way, for example) or constraints (the report has to be in a native Excel format, not tab- or column-separated). So at best, a 0.5 out of three here.

I'd like to get better by asking more questions rather than jumping to the conclusion that everything is okay. I think it will help to be more structured in my approach to briefings and back briefings, because that will prompt me to be more curious about what I'm saying and hearing. Finally, I'm going to try sharing more of my reactions rather than trying to look confident all the time. I hope this will help me work with Bobby and others more effectively, and avoid unpleasant surprises.

Improved Conversation

I checked with Bobby last week on the progress of the development team he works with. I wanted to handle this back briefing better, in line with what I learned from the earlier conversation. I asked a trusted friend to Role Play this discussion ahead of time, and that helped me be more curious as I went into the conversation.

Nicole and Bobby's Improved Conversation

What Nicole thought and felt	What Nicole and Bobby said
I wonder what he's prioritizing.	Nicole: You've got a lot of different projects in flight. Where do you plan to focus this week?
He's made a lot more progress than I realized. Um, wait—that's my twitch firing. I should check this out further.	Bobby: I'm thinking we're ready to finish the work on simplified configuration. I think I can get that done by Friday.
We haven't discussed how he'd present the findings from this investigation.	Nicole: Great! So how do you plan to present the results?
What?! It sounds like he's already moved on to implementation, and I haven't even seen the proposal yet.	Bobby: Last week I reviewed all the current config options, and the team has removed most of them. I expect I'll be able to demonstrate the new page with just five or six options.
Maybe he published his analysis and I missed it?	Nicole: Wait a minute—I'm confused. I was expecting you to examine and explain the need for each option, and I don't remember seeing a review document from you. Have you already done the analysis and moved onto implementation?
Oh dear! I thought I had been clear.	Bobby: What? I thought you wanted me to get rid of as many options as possible. We decided that Monday, when we said we'd simplify the config.
I don't want to be making arbitrary decisions.	Nicole: No, not really. What I wanted was to get your opinion on each option. Which of them do customers actually need and use?

	Bobby: Oh! Okay, well, that changes my plans for the week. We can pause the changes to the page, and I can focus on talking to more customers. We won't have the new page ready this week, though.
This sounds more like what I was expecting to hear.	
	Nicole: That's not a problem. It will be good to have greater confidence in our decision to keep, drop, or change the options, whichever we decide on.
I'm glad we had this conversation—we dodged a bullet here. We might have released the new page prematurely if we hadn't checked in.	

Having this conversation really helped both Bobby and me. Sharing the plan of action uncovered a gap in alignment: we both came into the conversation thinking we had a shared understanding of what "simplified configuration" meant, but we were actually far apart.

Previously I would have just assumed we agreed on this and accepted Bobby's assertion that the work would be done Friday. Instead, I asked Bobby for an account of what he planned to deliver and shared my emotions when I heard that he was planning something very different

As a result, our misalignment was in the open, and we could fix it before it did much damage. I still have some doubts about Bobby's listening skills, but I can see now that I was contributing to the problem. I think I can work with him much better in the future by using the Accountability Conversation.

Example Accountability Conversations

Grace and Lisa: Finding a Better Solution

Grace says, "From talking with our clients, we know that end-user engagement is important to them. We came up with a good solution to the problem, namely emailing a reminder at the start of the week to inactive users. We were almost ready to roll out the weekly reminders, and so we scheduled briefing calls with our key accounts to let them know what was coming. Most of them were very happy with our proposal, but one client, Lisa, had a very different reaction."

Grace and Lisa's Conversation

What Grace thought and felt	What Grace and Lisa said
I know Lisa has been concerned about engagement for a while. I expect she'll be happy with this, so I'll just explain what we're doing and why.	Grace: Hi Lisa, thanks for taking the time to hear about a change we are planning to implement. We are going to start sending an email on Mondays to any users who didn't log in the previous week. We are doing this in response to clients who are worried that end-users aren't always as engaged with the system as they'd like.
What?! You've complained to me about engagement again and again. I thought you'd be grateful.	Lisa: Ugh, please don't do that!
Weird, no other customer has objected to the emails. I'm pretty sure engagement is still a problem for you, but I should check.	Grace: Oh, that's surprising! I've spoken with several other clients, and you are the first person with that reaction. Looking at the latest usage report, I can see that 40% of your users are inactive. Do you see that as a problem?
Wow, sounds awful. No wonder she doesn't want us emailing users directly. And I'm glad she has an idea about what might work for them instead.	Lisa: Engagement is definitely something we want to improve. It's just that we already get so many emails sent from internal systems that it is impossible to keep up; and the last thing I want are complaints about getting even more. Could you send me a weekly report on inactive users instead? That would allow us to follow up internally.

	Grace: Absolutely. I can tell our team that you'd rather receive the information on inactive users instead of emailing the users directly. In our next quarterly review, we can talk about how those reports are working and if there's anything else we can do in the system to help.
This could be a good experiment. If it works, it might be something we can offer to other clients.	
	Lisa: That's great. I'm really glad you contacted me ahead of time rather than unleashing a flood of emails onto our users!
Me too!	

It is easy to believe that we understand both the problem and the solution when, in fact, we lack a key piece of knowledge. Grace had a solution that had been endorsed by several others for a problem she knew Lisa cared about; she couldn't have known that emails were an unacceptable approach in Lisa's organization. Being accountable means signaling our intent with others who will be impacted even when we think we are right. These opportunities come up most naturally inside the teams we work with daily. It is also worth looking for opportunities across departments and even across companies.

Andy and Wayne: Understanding Adaptation in the Moment

Andy says, "At the financial services company where I'm the Head of Engineering, when we perform an incident postmortem investigation, we are trying to understand not just what happened but also how the world looked to the people involved at the time. Our goal is to reconstruct a picture where the actions taken were the right ones; because no matter what we learn after the fact, we trust that the actions must have seemed right at the time. And whatever we do to make our systems resilient, it is the judgement and actions of the people in the moment that help us cope with the unexpected. Like when we recently lost data for one of our production systems and I asked Wayne, one of our system administrators, to account for his actions in restoring service."

Andy and Wayne's Conversation

What Andy thought and felt	What Andy and Wayne said
We have a normal process for restoring data. Why didn't they just use that?	Andy: Okay, that table was deleted and the service was offline. Why was it that you didn't use the normal documented backup procedure?
That's a good point. I'm sure we never expect this kind of partial failure.	Wayne: Well, that process assumes the entire database has been lost or corrupted. In our situation it was only one table, and as a result, most of the services were still operating normally. If we'd performed the normal disaster recovery process, it would have worked; but it also would have meant all the services would be offline for a day or more.
It must have been very stressful to realize none of the processes we'd practiced would apply.	Andy: I see, so you were in uncharted territory here.
I agree—that would have made the problem much worse.	Wayne: That's right! Of course we could have just followed the book, but that would have made things worse. It didn't seem like the right thing to do even though it was the documented process.
	Andy: So how did you figure out how to proceed?
I'm not sure I would have taken their approach, but they got their priorities right.	Wayne: Our first goal was to keep all the other services operating normally, and our second goal was to recover the lost table and restore the service that depends on it. We thought of multiple options for recovering the data, and not knowing which would be fastest, we started down several of those paths in parallel, with different people working on each one.

I'm glad Wayne was thinking creatively here. Playing it by the book would have meant hours of downtime and a much bigger headache.

Andy: That was sharp thinking! We should consider adding "try multiple solutions" to the runbook.

It is inevitable that things won't always go according to plan, so how will people respond when that happens? In Andy's organization, the message is that you are expected to use your professional judgement in the moment; and at the same time, you'll be expected to account for your reasoning after the fact. The goal is not to punish people for the unexpected; it is to learn as much as possible from the experience. This frees people to improvise and create better outcomes than a by-the-book mind-set would produce.

CASE STUDY: RESURRECTING THE DEAL

An Unexpected Opportunity

"I got it!" exclaimed Mike, bursting through the office door with a huge binder. "I got it! We're back in!"

Marcus, a product manager for London-based startup Arachnys, looked up skeptically. Mike had gone to see a major banking prospect to find out why they had said no to the company's anti-money-laundering product a few weeks before. Marcus had expected Mike to return with a list of reasons the competitor had won, grist for the product-development mill to help them win the next bid with someone else. What had Mike cooked up instead?

Mike excitedly spread out the contents of the binder. "These are the specifications the bank gave the other guys. Apparently, after they got the deal, the other company took one look at these and said they wouldn't commit to anything less than nine months for completion of the first version of the system, meeting all of these requirements. That's way too slow; so when I asked if we could have a look, they said, 'Sure!' and handed me this."

Marcus and his colleague, Annegret, also a PM, scanned the first few pages.

"Gee, did they leave out *anything*?" asked Annegret, with more than a hint of sarcasm. "Four types of authentication, integration endpoints for seventeen systems, and test data and protocols taking up—let me count—sixty-three pages. There are over a thousand line items in the requirements list."

"What were you thinking we'd do with this monster, Mike?" asked Marcus.

"Well, officially, all I said is that we'd give them our estimate," Mike replied. "But Benny, the big cheese who makes the decisions, walked me out—and at the door, I told him privately that we'd have a prototype for them soon."

Marcus and Annegret looked at each other, then asked simultaneously, with shocked expressions, "*How* soon?"

Mike smiled. "Um, six weeks?" he said, a little sheepishly.

The Impossible Becomes Possible

Marcus and Annegret could see immediately that the binder contained at least a year's worth of work for their small development team. Six weeks was certainly out of the question. But because Arachnys was the kind of place where questioning a briefing or an assignment was *de rigueur*, they didn't give up, and instead, began combing through the pages.

They found that many of the "requirements" were contradictory, a result of different departments adding their own wish lists to the document without regard to each other. Others were irrelevant to the regulatory requirement the system was supposed to address; and a few were downright impossible. Eliminating these nonsensical items reduced the demands substantially but still left hundreds of detailed items to be addressed.

They took another pass through the list, but this time, instead of eliminating features, they aimed to pick out only those that were absolutely necessary, to prove the bank could meet the regulatory standard. Like the Walking Skeleton of Chapter 6, these key features would form the backbone of the system and allow them to prove that a solution was possible, while providing a framework for continually adding more functionality. They circled each item that met their stringent test, then counted them up.

"Six!" said Annegret.

"I don't believe it," said Marcus. "Is that really everything?"

"We have been through every page," Annegret replied. "There's nothing else here."

"But will they buy it?"

"There's only one way to find out!"

The Moment of Truth

A couple of days later, surrounded by Chinese takeout boxes that testified to the midnight oil the two product managers had been burning, Annegret clicked "send" on their carefully crafted email to the bank. They'd analyzed each requirement and explained exactly why they'd whittled the list down to just six items. The email was their back briefing, responding to the bank's requirements by sharing their reasoning and describing how they would be accountable for delivering the much smaller scope they'd defined, with multiple deliveries in the runup to the six-week target.

Mike phoned as soon as the email hit his inbox, checking in from an industry conference. "This is great stuff! I'm sure they'll want us to build what you've proposed."

"I'm not so sure," replied Marcus in a tired voice. "We cut out nearly everything they asked for. The other company just said yes to everything. Why not stick with them?"

At that moment, Annegret's screen lit up with a new message. It was from Benny, the "big cheese."

"Go ahead," it said. "See you in six weeks."

Marcus and Annegret worked intensely with the developers to deliver the prototype, checking in often with the client as promised. Benny and his team were so delighted with the result and the clear accountability represented by the plan that they signed up for the full product, and rolled it out to hundreds of internal users.

Afterward, Marcus had the opportunity to ask Benny, "Why did you decide to go with us?"

Benny was clear in his response. "Because you said no. You thought about what you could and could not deliver, and you shared your reasoning with us. And then you delivered what you committed to. That convinced me I could trust you to follow through on the rest of the project."

The Accountability Conversation had come up aces for both Arachnys and their client.

Conclusion: Applying the Accountability Conversation

In this chapter, you learned to *foster accountability* by adopting Theory Y, to identify and use *constraints and freedoms* for a planned action by using briefings and back briefings, and to *render an account* by signaling your intent both broadly and clearly. Being accountable for successes as well as failures allows you to learn effectively from experience and promotes the productive reasoning that drives your conversational transformation. You can use the Accountability Conversation in many ways, including the following:

- An ***executive leader*** can render an account of her strategic actions to those in her organization, helping them align with product and company goals.
- A ***team lead*** can brief team members on actions like testing a new feature or performing a penetration test, and have confidence in accurate execution through back briefings.
- An ***individual contributor*** can discover internal commitment and drive by seeing that his peers and managers view him as motivated and capable, perhaps by trusting him to try a new library or experiment with a creative redesign.

Conclusion

How to Keep Learning

Congratulations! If you've finished this book (instead of just flipping to the conclusion) and tried holding some or all of the Five Conversations, then you have overcome your dread of difficult conversations, have undertaken difficult emotional work, and are on the road to developing the five key attributes of high-performing teams: high Trust, low Fear, clear Why, definite Commitment, and solid Accountability. You have mastered a wide array of skills and techniques that contribute to successful conversations, including Test-Driven Development for People, Coherence Busting, Joint Design, the Walking Skeleton, and Directed Opportunism. These are fantastic accomplishments!

But we have challenging news for you. Though you've come a long way, there are still years of practice ahead of you. That's because none of the Five Conversations ever end. After you build Trust using TDD for People, you will need to keep aligning your stories as circumstances evolve and your view of the other person changes. After you define a clear Why with Joint Design, the market or your company will shift, and you will have to rebuild another Why. You and your team will want to discuss Accountability with each other throughout your time together, rendering meaningful accounts over and over as you fulfill your commitments to each other.

The Road Never Ends

As we argued throughout this book, a conversational transformation is the way out of the feature factory that traps so many Agile, Lean, and DevOps teams. Now that you know this, we're sure you will drive many conversational transformations in teams and organizations you work in. This means you will have the opportunity to keep improving your conversation technique throughout your life. As with any other skill, such as playing an instrument or practicing a sport, continued practice allows us to perform with more grace and style. It also challenges us by showing us that further improvement is always possible. Even after studying these methods for over ten years, both of us continue to make and discover new mistakes, which also allows us to learn new skills and invent new techniques. In the morning, we may have a wonderful, relationship-building conversation, but that afternoon, we may stumble through an acrimonious discussion that leaves everyone frustrated. We have experienced the real value in continuing to practice methods like conversational analysis, and even more value in patient friends willing to practice and role play with us. The failed conversations may be painful, but they give us the greatest opportunity to develop our most important skills.

Start a Learning Group

The most useful resource you have in improving your conversations is the help of other people who are also looking to improve the same skills. And so our final recommendation to you is that you find others in your organization or your community who can work with you regularly to jointly improve their mastery of the techniques in this book—others who will join you in following Argyris's strategy of using conversations to investigate and improve your organization's performance.

It is a quirk of human nature and the result of our cognitive biases that the mistakes of other people are easier to spot than our own. Your fellow learners will spot alternatives in your discussions that you missed, and you will do the same for them. A learning group also offers a good space for deliberate practice, where you can try applying the techniques in the room and get immediate feedback from other people on how it felt for them.

Our advice for starting a learning group is to start simple and to focus on building the habit of regular practice. Begin by asking each person to read out a conversation analysis, and discuss each person's conversation with the group. Creating and scoring your conversations in advance will help you get more out of your time. However, it is better to meet without preparation—to do the conversation analysis in the session—than to skip the session; even the smallest amount of work will be rewarded. We have held successful practice sessions in groups from two to twenty, with coworkers and friends and people who started as strangers, and discussed conversations with bosses, colleagues, neighbors, spouses, parents, roommates, and more. Every conversation offers the opportunity to improve if you are looking for it.

As you become more comfortable with your learning group, you may want to study articles or videos, or undertake other deliberate practices to help you improve further. One group we know is working its way through the Agile Manifesto principles one at a time; another meets monthly to practice new techniques, like nonviolent communication[1] and relationship journaling.[2] The "Further Reading and Resources" section at the end of this book (page 189) will give you many ideas and sources for additional work, including ways to keep in touch with both of us online on the companion website and podcast for this book.

Dry Kitesurfing

After a long lunch with much discussion of conversation techniques from this book, a client of ours said, "I feel like I've just had a lecture on kitesurfing, but I didn't get wet." You can study all the theoretical knowledge you want, but it will do you no good at all without getting in the water and falling off the board a few times.

We invite you to dive in and practice the conversation techniques we have shared with you on a regular basis. The rewards are enormous.

Keep talking,
Jeffrey and Squirrel

Conversation Scoring: A Handy Guide

Once you've recorded your conversation in the two-column format, follow these steps to Reflect on your curiosity, transparency, conversational patterns, and use of key skills we describe in the book.

1. *Curiosity*: Determine your Question Fraction.
    a. Circle all the question marks in the right-hand column.
    b. Count the number of questions that were *genuine*.
    c. Write a fraction: $\frac{\textit{Genuine Questions}}{\textit{Total Questions}}$.
    d. For maximum curiosity, you want to see lots of questions (a large denominator), with most of them genuine (a large numerator).
2. *Transparency*: Find unexpressed ideas.
    a. Underline thoughts and feelings in the left-hand column that do not appear in the right-hand column.
    b. You have been very transparent if you have expressed most of your thinking and your emotions (that is, if you have few underlined sentences in the left-hand column).
3. *Patterns*: Find triggers, tells, and twitches.
    a. Circle and label *triggers* that cause you to react strongly, *tells* that signal a lack of transparency or curiosity, and *twitches* that represent default responses.

b. You probably can't avoid the automatic responses you identify here, but you can learn to detect them as they happen. You are doing well if you note your patterns in real time, either in your left-hand column or in your dialogue.

4. *Skills*: Test for specific skills you are trying to improve (choose from the list of skills below, and only work on one at a time).
   a. *TDD for People*: Label your statements and questions in either column with the rung from the Ladder of Inference to which they belong. You're doing well if you're establishing a shared understanding of the lower rungs of the Ladder before debating items near the top the Ladder.
   b. *Coherence Busting*: Count the unsupported conclusions in the left-hand column. Aim for a low score—ideally, none!
   c. *Joint Design*: Award a point for each of the five elements of Joint Design that you observe: inclusivity, asking genuine questions, inviting opposing views, timeboxing, and using a decision-making rule. Aim for five out of five.
   d. *Agreeing on Meaning*: Circle the important words in both columns, then count the number that have confirmed, shared meanings. Create a fraction: $\frac{\textit{Words with Comfirmed, Shared Meanings}}{\textit{Important Words}}$. Ideally, this fraction will be equal to 1 (the numerator equals the denominator).
   e. *Briefing and Back Briefing*: As appropriate, score yourself out of three: for a briefing, look for outcome, constraints, and freedoms; for a back briefing, watch for action, reasoning, and confirmation. Your goal should be a score of $\frac{3}{3}$.

Further Reading and Resources

There is a lot of rich literature about communication; and we share some of our favorite sources below.

Articles

The following articles describe tools for analyzing conversations, only some of which were included in this book.

- *Eight Behaviours for Smarter Teams* by Roger Schwarz (https://www.csu.edu.au/__data/assets/pdf_file/0008/917018/Eight-Behaviors-for-Smarter-Teams-2.pdf)
- "Putting the 'Relational' Back in Human Relationships" by Diana McLain Smith (https://thesystemsthinker.com/putting-the-relational-back-in-human-relationships/)
- "To the Rescue" by Roger Martin from the *Stanford Social Innovation Review* (https://ssir.org/articles/entry/to_the_rescue)
- "Skilled Incompetence" by Chris Argyris from the *Harvard Business Review* (https://hbr.org/1986/09/skilled-incompetence)

Books

Difficult Conversations by Bruce Patton, Douglas Stone, and Sheila Heen is a gentle introduction to the techniques we describe in *Agile Conversations*.

The Skilled Facilitator by Roger Schwarz and *Discussing the Undiscussable* by Bill Noonan are more advanced guides to conversational analysis, covering many applications and including real-world examples.

The Elephant in the Room by Diana McLain Smith and *The Responsibility Virus* by Roger Martin cover specific applications of conversational techniques to complex business relationships, such as those burdened with a long history of poor interaction or with confusion over roles and responsibilities.

Action Science by Chris Argyris, Robert Putnam, and Diana McLain Smith is the seminal work on the Action Science methods that provided the bedrock for this book and several of the other resources in this list. It is more academic and theoretical than other writings cited here, and has the additional virtue of being freely available online.

I'm Right, You're Wrong, Now What?: Break the Impasse and Get What You Need by Dr. Xavier Amador describes the model he developed while providing therapy for people in denial to the general public: LEAP (Listen-Empathize-Agree-Partner). This approach is conversational and, we believe, is both similar to and applicable for the methods we describe in this book.

Nonviolent Communication: A Language of Life by Marshall B. Rosenberg, PhD, is more than an approach to communication; it is a philosophy for living. However, even people skeptical of this philosophy can find some very useful exercises to reflect on their communication and their mind-set.

Video and Audio

Every week on the *Troubleshooting Agile* podcast (https://troubleshootingagile.com), we discuss relevant, current topics in Agile, Lean, and DevOps teams, offering ideas and solutions for improving delivery and communication in software teams.

The weekly *Feeling Good* podcast by Dr. David Burns (https://feelinggood.com/list-of-feeling-good-podcasts/) regularly provides excellent real-life examples of how changing conversations changes relationships. Particularly relevant are the episodes covering The Five Secrets of Communication and the Interpersonal Model.

The companion website for this book, ConversationalTransformation.com, has follow-up materials, videos, a mailing list to join, and much more.

In Person

The London Organisational Learning Meetup, (https://www.meetup.com/London-Action-Science-Meetup) meets monthly in London. It is run by Jeffrey Fredrick, and is an excellent opportunity to practice and improve your conversations with others who are interested in changing culture.

References

Adžić, Gojko. *Specification by Example: How Successful Teams Deliver the Right Software*. Shelter Island, New York: Manning, 2011.

Allspaw, John, and Paul Hammond. "10+ Deploys per Day: Dev and Ops Cooperation at Flickr." SlideShare.net. Posted by John Allspaw, June 23, 2009. https://www.slideshare.net/jallspaw/10-deploys-per-day-dev-and-ops-cooperation-at-flickr.

Anderson, David J. *Kanban: Successful Evolutionary Change for Your Technology Business*. Sequim, WA: Blue Hole Press, 2010.

Appleton, Brad. "The First Thing to Build Is TRUST!" *Brad Appleton's ACME Blog*. February 3, 2005. http://bradapp.blogspot.com/2005/02/first-thing-to-build-is-trust.html.

Argyris, Chris. *Organizational Traps: Leadership, Culture, Organizational Design*. Oxford: Oxford University Press, 2010.

Argyris, Chris. "Skilled Incompetence." *Harvard Business Review* (September, 1986): hbr.org/1986/09/skilled-incompetence.

Argyris, Chris, Robert Putnam, and Diana McLain Smith. *Action Science: Concepts, Methods, and Skills for Research and Intervention*. San Francisco, CA: Jossey-Bass, 1985.

Argyris, Chris, and Donald Schön. *Theory in Practice: Increasing Professional Effectiveness*. San Francisco, CA: Jossey-Bass, 1974.

Ayer, Elizabeth. "Don't Ask Forgiveness, Radiate Intent." Medium.com. June 27, 2019. https://medium.com/@ElizAyer/dont-ask-forgiveness-radiate-intent-d36fd22393a3.

Beck, Kent. *Extreme Programming Explained: Embrace Change*. Reading, MA: Addison-Wesley, 2000.

Beck, Kent. *Test-Driven Development: By Example*. Boston, MA: Addison-Wesley, 2003.

Beck, Kent, et al. "Manifesto for Agile Software Development." AgileManifesto.org. 2001. https://agilemanifesto.org.

Beck, Kent, et al. "Principles Behind the Agile Manifesto." AgileManifesto.org. 2001. https://agilemanifesto.org/principles.html.

Brown, Brené. *Rising Strong: How the Ability to Reset Transforms the Way We Live, Love, Parent, and Lead*. New York: Spiegel & Grau, 2015.

Bungay, Stephen. *The Art of Action: How Leaders Close the Gaps between Plans, Actions and Results*. New York: Hachette, 2011.

Burns, David. *Feeling Good Together: The Secret to Making Troubled Relationships Work*. New York: Random House, 2010.

Center for Nonviolent Communication. "Feelings Inventory." Accessed September 23, 2019. https://www.cnvc.org/training/resource/feelings-inventory.

Cockburn, Alistair. *Agile Software Development: The Cooperative Game*, 2nd ed. Boston, MA: Addison-Wesley, 2007.

Cockburn, Alistair. "Characterizing People as Non-Linear, First-Order Components in Software Development." *Humans and Technology. HaT Technical Report* 1999.03, October 21, 1999. http://web.archive.org/web/20140329203655/http://alistair.cockburn.us/Characterizing+people+as+non-linear,+first-order+components+in+software+development.

Cockburn, Alastair. "Heart of Agile." HeartofAgile.com. 2016. https://heartofagile.com.

Coleman, Mark. "A Re-Imagining of the Term; 'Full-Stack Developer.'" Amsterdam DevOpsDays 2015 proposal. Accessed Feruary 3, 2020. https://legacy.devopsdays.org/events/2015-amsterdam/proposals/mark-robert-coleman__a-re-imagining-of-the-term-full-stack-developer/.

Cutler, John. "12 Signs You're Working in a Feature Factory," *Hacker Noon* (blog). Medium.com. November 16, 2016. https://medium.com/hackernoon/12-signs-youre-working-in-a-feature-factory-44a5b938d6a2.

Debois, Patrick. "Agile Operations—Xpdays France 2009." SlideShare .net. November 27, 2009. https://www.slideshare.net/jedi4ever/agile -operations-xpdays-france-2009.

Dennett, Daniel. *From Bacteria to Bach and Back: The Evolution of Minds*. New York: W. W. Norton, 2017.

Derby, Esther, and Diana Larsen. *Agile Retrospectives: Making Good Teams Great*. Raleigh, NC: Pragmatic Bookshelf, 2006.

Duff, John D., and Louis E. Dietrich. Dehydrated flour mix and process of making the same. US Patent 2,016,320, filed June 13, 1933, and issued October 8, 1935, https://pdfpiw.uspto.gov/.piw?Docid=02016320.

Edmondson, Amy. *Teaming: How Organizations Learn, Innovate, and Compete in the Knowledge Economy*. Hoboken, NJ: Jossey-Bass, 2012.

Financial Times. "FT Tops One Million Paying Readers." *Financial Times*. April 1, 2019. https://aboutus.ft.com/en-gb/announcements/ft-tops-one-million -one-million-paying-readers/.

Fisher, Roger, William Ury, and Bruce Patton. *Getting to Yes: Negotiating Agreement without Giving In*. New York: Houghton Mifflin, 1991.

Fitz, Timothy. "Continuous Deployment at IMVU: Doing the Impossible Fifty Times a Day." *Timothy Fitz* (blog). February 10, 2009. http://timothyfitz .com/2009/02/10/continuous-deployment-at-imvu-doing-the-impossible -fifty-times-a-day/.

Forsgren, Nicole, Jez Humble, and Gene Kim. *Accelerate: The Science of Lean Software and DevOps: Building and Scaling High Performing Technology Organizations*. Portland, OR: IT Revolution, 2018.

Fowler, Martin. "Writing the Agile Manifesto." MartinFowler.com (blog). July 9, 2006. https://martinfowler.com/articles/agileStory.html.

Goldratt, Eliyahu M. and Jeff Cox. *The Goal*. Aldershot, England: Gower Publishing, 1984.

Griffin, Dale, and Lee Ross. "Subjective Construal, Social Inference, and Human Misunderstanding." *Advances in Experimental Social Psychology 24* (1991): 319–359.

Harari, Yuval Noah. *Homo Deus: A Brief History of Tomorrow*. London: Harvill Secker, 2015.

Harari, Yuval Noah. *Sapiens: A Brief History of Humankind*. New York: Harper, 2014.

Highsmith, Jim. "History: The Agile Manifesto." AgileManifesto.org. 2001. https://agilemanifesto.org/history.html.

Hihn, Jairus, et al. "ASCoT: The Official Release; A Web-Based Flight Software Estimation Tool." Presentation. 2017 NASA Cost Symposium, NASA Headquarters, Washington, DC. https://www.nasa.gov/sites/default/files/atoms/files/19_costsymp-ascot-hihn_tagged.pdf.

Humble, Jez, Joanne Molesky, and Barry O'Reilly. *Lean Enterprise: How High Performance Organizations Innovate at Scale*. Boston, MA: O'Reilly, 2015.

Humphrey, Watts S. *Characterizing the Software Process: A Maturity Framework*. Pittsburgh, PA: Software Engineering Institute, Carnegie Mellon University, 1987. ftp://ftp.cert.org/pub/documents/87.reports/pdf/tr11.pdf.

Kahneman, Daniel. *Thinking, Fast and Slow*. New York: Farrar, Straus and Giroux, 2011.

King, Martin Luther, Jr. "I Have a Dream." Speech. Washington, DC, August 28, 1963. American Rhetoric, mp3 recording. Last updated February 14, 2019. http://www.americanrhetoric.com/speeches/mlkihaveadream.htm.

Kurtz, Cynthia F. and David J. Snowden. "The New Dynamics of Strategy: Sense-Making in a Complex and Complicated World." *IBM Systems Journal* 42, no. 3 (2003): 462–483.

Latané, Bibb, and John M. Darley. *The Unresponsive Bystander: Why Doesn't He Help*? Upper Saddle River, NJ: Prentice-Hall, 1970.

Lencioni, Patrick. *The Five Dysfunctions of a Team: A Leadership Fable*. New York: Wiley & Sons, 2010.

Martirosyan, Arthur. "Getting to 'Yes' in Iraq." Mercy Corps blog. July 1, 2009. https://www.mercycorps.org/articles/iraq/getting-yes-iraq.

McGregor, Douglas. *The Human Side of Enterprise, Annotated Edition*. New York: McGraw-Hill, 2006.

Mezak, Steve. "The Origins of DevOps: What's in a Name?" DevOps.com. January 25, 2018. https://devops.com/the-origins-of-devops-whats-in-a-name/.

Murphy, Gregory. *The Big Book of Concepts*. Boston: MIT Press, 2004.

NASA. *Report to the President by the Presidential Commission on the Space Shuttle* Challenger *Accident*. Washington, DC: NASA, 1986.

Nelson, Daniel, ed. *A Mental Revolution: Scientific Management Since Taylor*. Columbus, OH: Ohio State University Press, 1992.

Park, Michael Y. "A History of the Cake Mix, the Invention that Redefined Baking." *Bon Appétit* blog. September 26, 2013. https://www.bonappetit.com/entertaining-style/pop-culture/article/cake-mix-history.

Pflaeging, Niels. "Why We Cannot Learn a Damn Thing from Toyota, or Semco," LinkedIn, September 13, 2015. https://www.linkedin.com/pulse/why-we-cannot-learn-damn-thing-from-semco-toyota-niels-pflaeging/.

Poole, Reginald. *The Exchequer in the Twelfth Century*. Oxford: University of Oxford, 1911. https://socialsciences.mcmaster.ca/econ/ugcm/3ll3/poole/exchequer12c.pdf.

Poppendieck, Mary, and Tom Poppendieck. *Lean Software Development: An Agile Toolkit*. Boston: Addison Wesley, 2003.

Reinertsen, Donald. "An Introduction to Second Generation Lean Product Development." Presentation. Lean Kanban France 2015. https://www.slideshare.net/don600/reinertsen-lk-france-2015-11-415.

Ries, Eric. *The Lean Startup: How Today's Entrepreneurs Use Continuous Innovation to Create Radically Successful Businesses*. London: Penguin, 2011.

Rogers, Bruce. "Innovation Leaders: Inc.Digital's Michael Gale On Digital Transformation." *Forbes*. January 16, 2018. https://www.forbes.com/sites/brucerogers/2018/01/16/innovation-leaders-inc-digitals-michael-gale-on-digital-transformation/#45d9ee157693.

Rogers, Bruce. "Why 84% of Companies Fail at Digital Transformation." *Forbes*. January 7, 2016. https://www.forbes.com/sites/brucerogers/2016/01/07/why-84-of-companies-fail-at-digital-transformation/#5d0b0759397b.

Roos, Daniel, James Womack, and Daniel Jones. *The Machine That Changed the World: The Story of Lean Production*. New York: Harper Perennial, 1991.

Rosenberg, Marshall. *Nonviolent Communication: A Language of Life*, 3rd ed. Encinitas, CA: Puddledancer Press, 2015.

Schwarz, Roger. "Eight Behaviors for Smarter Teams." Roger Schwarz & Associates website. 2013. https://www.csu.edu.au/__data/assets/pdf_file/0008/917018 /Eight-Behaviors-for-Smarter-Teams-2.pdf.

Schwarz, Roger. *Smart Leaders, Smarter Teams: How You and Your Team Get Unstuck to Get Results*. San Francisco, CA: Jossey-Bass, 2013.

Senge, Peter. *The Fifth Discipline: The Art and Practice of the Learning Organization*. New York: Currency Doubleday, 1990.

Sheridan, Richard. *Joy, Inc.: How We Built a Workplace People Love*. New York: Penguin Group, 2013.

Shipler, David. "Reagan and Gorbachev Sign Missile Treaty and Vow to Work for Greater Reductions." NYTimes. December 9, 1987. https://www.nytimes.com/1987/12/09/politics/reagan-and-gorbachev-sign-missile-treaty-and-vow-to-work-for.html.

Shipman, Anna. "After the Launch: The Difficult Teenage Years." Presentation. Continuous Lifecycle 2019. https://www.slideshare.net/annashipman/after-the-launch-the-difficult-teenage-years.

Shipman, Anna. "How Do You Delegate to a Group of People?" *Anna Shipman* (blog). June 21, 2019. https://www.annashipman.co.uk/jfdi/delegating-to-a-team.html.

Silvers, Emma. "A New Guest at Your House Show: The Middleman." KQED website. April 28, 2017. https://www.kqed.org/arts/13114272/sofar-sounds-house-shows-airbnb-middleman.

Sinek, Simon. "How Great Leaders Inspire Action." Filmed September 2009 in Newcastle, WY. TED video, 17:49. https://www.ted.com/talks/simon_sinek_how_great_leaders_inspire_action.

Sinek, Simon. *Start with Why: How Great Leaders Inspire Everyone to Take Action*. London: Penguin, 2011.

The Standish Group. *The CHAOS Report: 1994*. Boston, MA: The Standish Group, 1995. https://www.standishgroup.com/sample_research_files/chaos_report_1994.pdf.

Travaglia, Simon. "Data Centre: BOFH." *The Register*. 2000–19, https://www.theregister.co.uk/data_centre/bofh/.

Travaglia, Simon "The Revised, King James Prehistory of BOFH. Revision: 6f." *The Bastard Operator from Hell* (blog). Accessed October 23, 2019. http://bofharchive.com/BOFH-Prehistory.html.

Vaughan, Diane. *The* Challenger *Launch Decision: Risky Technology, Culture, and Deviance at NASA*. Chicago, IL: University of Chicago Press, 1996.

Weinberg, Gerard M. *The Secrets of Consulting: A Guide to Giving and Getting Advice Successfully*. Gerard M. Weinberg, 2011.

West, Dave. "Water-Scrum-Fall Is the Reality of Agile for Most Organizations Today." *Forrester*. July 26, 2011. https://www.verheulconsultants.nl/water-scrum-fall_Forrester.pdf.

Notes

Introduction

1. Lencioni, *Five Dysfunctions of a Team*, "Exhibition."
2. Lencioni, *Five Dysfunctions of a Team*, "Understanding and Overcoming the Five Dysfunctions."
3. Coleman, "A Re-Imagining of the Term."
4. Lencioni, *Five Dysfunctions of a Team*.
5. Sinek, *Start with Why*.

Chapter 1

1. Michael Gale, as quoted in Rogers, "Why 84% of Companies Fail."
2. Michael Gale, as quoted in Rogers, "Innovation Leaders."
3. Cutler, "12 Signs You're Working in a Feature Factory."
4. Nelson, *A Mental Revolution*, 5–11.
5. The Standish Group, *The CHAOS Report: 1994*, 3.
6. Humphrey, *Characterizing the Software Process*, 2.
7. Cockburn, "Characterizing People as Non-Linear, First-Order Components."
8. Cockburn, "Characterizing People as Non-Linear, First-Order Components."
9. Cockburn, "Characterizing People as Non-Linear, First-Order Components."
10. Roos, Womack, and Jones, *The Machine That Changed the World*, 52.
11. Fitz, "Continuous Deployment at IMVU."
12. Highsmith, "History: The Agile Manifesto."
13. Highsmith, "History: The Agile Manifesto."

14. Fowler, "Writing the Agile Manifesto."
15. Beck, et al., "Manifesto for Agile Software Development."
16. Beck, et al., "Principles Behind the Agile Manifesto."
17. Poppendieck and Poppendieck, *Lean Software Development*, xxv.
18. Poppendieck and Poppendieck, *Lean Software Development*, 101.
19. Debois, "Agile Operations."
20. Mezak, "The Origins of DevOps."
21. Allspaw and Hammond, "10+ Deploys per Day."
22. Allspaw and Hammond, "10+ Deploys per Day."
23. Travaglia, "The Revised, King James Prehistory of BOFH."
24. Eric Minick, private correspondence with the authors, July 12, 2019.
25. West, "Water-Scrum-Fall Is the Reality."
26. Sheridan, *Joy, Inc.*, 19.
27. Pflaeging, "Why We Cannot Learn a Damn Thing."
28. Kurtz and Snowden, "The New Dynamics of Strategy," 462–483.
29. Kurtz and Snowden, "The New Dynamics of Strategy," 469.

Chapter 2

1. Harari, *Sapiens*, 20.
2. Dennett, *From Bacteria to Bach and Back*, Chapter 14.
3. Harari, *Sapiens*, Chapter 2.
4. Harari, *Homo Deus*, 158.
5. Forsgren, Humble, and Kim, *Accelerate*, 31.
6. Argyris, Putnam, and McLain Smith, *Action Science*, 79.
7. Argyris and Schön, *Theory in Practice*.
8. Argyris and Schön, *Theory in Practice*, 6–7.
9. Argyris, Putnam, and McLain Smith, *Action Science*, 81–83.
10. Argyris, *Organizational Traps*, 61.
11. Argyris, *Organizational Traps*, 17.
12. Argyris, Putnam, and McLain Smith, *Action Science*, 98–102.
13. Argyris, Putnam, and McLain Smith, *Action Science*, 90–99.
14. Argyris, "Skilled Incompetence," 5.
15. Argyris, Putnam, and McLain Smith, *Action Science*, 88–98.
16. Cockburn, "Characterizing People as Non-Linear."
17. Cockburn, "Characterizing People as Non-Linear."
18. Loosely based on Schwarz, "Eight Behaviors for Smarter Teams."
19. Rosenberg, *Nonviolent Communication*, 115.
20. Center for Nonviolent Communication, "Feelings Inventory."
21. Rosenberg, *Nonviolent Communication*, 93.
22. Argyris, Putnam, and McLain Smith, *Action Science*, 98.

Chapter 3

1. Appleton, "The First Thing to Build Is TRUST."
2. Brown, *Rising Strong*, 86.
3. Kahneman, *Thinking, Fast and Slow*, 85.
4. Beck, *Test-Driven Development*, xvi.
5. Argyris, Putnam, and McLain Smith, *Action Science*, 57.
6. Argyris, Putnam, and McLain Smith, *Action Science*, 58.

Chapter 4

1. Edmondson, *Teaming*, Chapter 4.
2. Edmondson, *Teaming*, Chapter 4.
3. Beck, *Extreme Programming Explained*, 33.
4. Allspaw and Hammond, "10+ Deploys per Day."
5. Bibb Latané and John M. Darley, *Unresponsive Bystander*, 46.
6. Vaughan, *The* Challenger *Launch Decision*.
7. NASA, *Report of the Presidential Commission*, Appendix F.
8. Kahneman, *Thinking, Fast and Slow*, Chapter 1.
9. Kahneman, *Thinking, Fast and Slow*, 85.

Chapter 5

1. Sinek, "How Great Leaders Inspire Action."
2. Sinek, *Start with Why*, 94.
3. King, "I Have a Dream."
4. Martirosyan, "Getting to 'Yes' in Iraq"; Fisher, Ury, and Patton, *Getting to Yes*, 23.
5. Argyris, "Skilled Incompetence," 5.
6. Senge, *The Fifth Discipline*, 185.
7. Park, "A History of the Cake Mix."
8. Duff and Dietrich, Dehydrated flour mix.
9. Gerald M. Weinberg, *The Secrets of Consulting*, 177.
10. Gerald M. Weinberg, *The Secrets of Consulting*, 177.
11. Schwarz, "Eight Behaviors for Smarter Teams."

Chapter 6

1. Schwarz, *Smart Leaders, Smarter Teams*, 99.
2. Murphy, *The Big Book of Concepts*.
3. Adžić, *Specification by Example*.
4. Silvers, "A New Guest at Your House Show."
5. Cockburn, *Agile Software Development*, 357.
6. Hihn, et al., "ASCoT: The Official Release."
7. Shipman, "How Do You Delegate to a Group of People?"

8. *Financial Times*, "FT Tops One Million Paying Readers."
9. Shipman, "How Do You Delegate to a Group of People?"
10. Shipman, "How Do You Delegate to a Group of People?"
11. Shipman, "How Do You Delegate to a Group of People?"
12. Shipman, "How Do You Delegate to a Group of People?"
13. Shipman, "After the Launch: The Difficult Teenage Years."
14. Shipman, "How Do You Delegate to a Group of People?"

Chapter 7

1. Merriam-Webster Dictionary, s.v. "account," accessed July 20, 2019, https://www.merriam-webster.com/dictionary/account.
2. Poole, *The Exchequer in the Twelfth Century*, 128.
3. Poole, *The Exchequer in the Twelfth Century*, 139.
4. Poole, *The Exchequer in the Twelfth Century*, 100.
5. Poole, *The Exchequer in the Twelfth Century*, 34.
6. Poole, *The Exchequer in the Twelfth Century*, 127.
7. Poole, *The Exchequer in the Twelfth Century*, 107.
8. McGregor, *The Human Side of Enterprise*, 43 and 59.
9. Pflaeging, "Why We Cannot Learn a Damn Thing."
10. Griffin and Ross, "Subjective Construal," 319–359.
11. Bungay, *The Art of Action*.
12. Bungay, *The Art of Action*, 50.
13. Bungay, *The Art of Action*, 123–130.
14. Reinertsen, "An Introduction to Second Generation Lean Product Development."
15. Bungay, *The Art of Action*, 123–130.
16. Ayer, "Don't Ask Forgiveness, Radiate Intent."
17. Shipler, "Reagan and Gorbachev Sign Missile Treaty."
18. Cockburn, *Agile Software Development*, 98.

Conclusion

1. Rosenberg, *Nonviolent Communication*.
2. Burns, *Feeling Good Together*.

Acknowledgments

This book is built on a foundation formed of many conversations—some joyful, some painful, and *all* sources of learning. Here are some of the people whose conversations with us have helped us grow and learn so far, and for whom we are very grateful:

Benjamin Mitchell, who introduced us to the work of Chris Argryis, and patiently worked with us as we learned conversational analysis and much more. Waseem Taj, Andy Parker, Jamie Mill, and Lisa Miller, who joined us in learning how to analyze conversations and to lose our fear of difficult interactions. Rich Koppel and Colin Berthoud, the founders of TIM Group, and the many employees there who worked with us (especially with Jeffrey), to experiment with growing a learning organization based on transparency and curiosity. Steve Freeman, who encouraged us to tell the story of the changes at TIM Group (this book doesn't tell that story, but it does share the conversations behind those changes).

The participants in our CTO Mentoring Circles and the London Organisational Learning Meetup, which served as testbeds for many of the concepts herein.

Chris Argyris and Donald Schön, whose theories underpin so much of this book. Also those who developed their ideas, including Philip McArthur, Robert Putnam, and Diana McLain Smith of Action Design, and Roger Schwarz, whose Eight Behaviors helped us greatly in our early conversations.

Patrick Lencioni, whose model of hierarchical dysfunctions informed the order of our conversations. Amy Edmondson, who brought "psychological safety" to our vocabulary. Simon Sinek, who explained the value of Why. Stephen Bungay, who showed the value of briefing and back briefing. Brené Brown, who helped us to put the story we were telling ourselves into words. Dr. David Burns, who helped us understand the fractal nature of conversations—that we create our interpersonal reality.

Alistair Cockburn, Kent Beck, and others of the early Agile software development community who pioneered the radical idea that relationships matter, back when both of us were still trapped in the software factory. Mary Poppendieck, Tom Poppendieck, Eric Ries, and others who helped bring Lean thinking to the software world. Patrick Debois, John Allspaw, and Paul Hammond, who helped shatter the silo that remained at the last mile, and who ensured that DevOps was about culture and not just tools.

Geckoboard (including Paul Joyce and Leo Cassarani), Unmade Ltd., and Arachnys, each of whom kindly allowed us to include the details of their work with us.

Anna Shipman, whose insightful blog post became a case study.

Sofar Sounds, who kindly allowed us to include a story about them.

Sergiusz Bleja, who allowed us to include a case study we created with him.

The Belgian Federal Pensions Service, Thierry de Pauw, and Tom Jans, who kindly allowed us to include details from one of their projects as a case study.

Elisabeth Hendrickson, whose excitement about this material led her to introduce us to IT Revolution, and who additionally suggested we add "twitch" to our analysis repertoire.

Mark Coleman, who provided very useful advice at crucial stages and gave us the concept of "difficult emotional work."

Eric Minick, whose perspective on how far we've come was very helpful.

Chris Matts and Cirilo Wortel, who shared stories and ideas while the book was taking shape.

Ian Ozsvald, who gave us invaluable advice and contacts at a very early stage.

Gojko Adžić, who shared much information and advice about his publishing and consulting experience, and whose joyful approach to testing and product management has been a pleasure to observe.

Paul Julius, whose suggestion that we create a conference led to Squirrel and Jeffrey meeting (and so much more). And the attendees of that conference, the Continuous Integration and Testing Conference (CITCON), to whom we have been promising this book for many years.

Alan Weiss and Gerald Weinberg, whose writings on publishing and promoting books were inspirational for us throughout.

Laurel Ruma and Melissa Duffield, who helped us solidify our very loose initial ideas for what became this book.

Anna Noak, whose patient feedback throughout the proposal and writing stages was vital to creating the finished product, and the many others at IT Revolution who contributed to this book in a plentitude of ways.

Listeners to our podcast, *Troubleshooting Agile*, who provided stories, advice, and a sounding board for many of our ideas; and Michelle Choi and Laura Stack, who make sure the podcast engine is always running.

The many people and teams who allowed us to coach them and learn from them over the last two decades.

Jerry Shurman and Joe Buhler, who taught Squirrel to take joy in intellectual endeavors.

Pat Yanez, Ron Fredrick, and Marilyn Fredrick, who gave Jeffrey the background to attempt the difficult.

Thanks to Robert Schuessler for keen eyes and a quick turnaround.

And finally, our families—Andreas, Anton, Eliana, Emeline, Leanne, Lisa, and Star—whose patience was tested, who never stopped believing in us, and whose support was invaluable.

About the Authors

Douglas Squirrel has been coding for forty years and has led software teams for twenty. He uses the power of conversations to create dramatic productivity gains in technology organizations of all sizes. Squirrel's experience includes growing software teams as a CTO in startups, from fintech to e-commerce; consulting on product improvement at over sixty organizations in the UK, US, and Europe; and coaching a wide variety of leaders in improving their conversations, aligning to business goals, and creating productive conflict. He lives in Frogholt, England, in a timber-framed cottage built in the year 1450.

Jeffrey Fredrick is an internationally recognized expert in software development and has over twenty-five years' experience covering both sides of the business/technology divide. An early adopter of XP and Agile practices, Jeffrey has been a conference speaker in the US, Europe, India, and Japan. Through his work on the pioneering open-source project CruiseControl, and through his role as co-organizer of the Continuous Integration and Testing Conference (CITCON), he has had a global impact on software development. Jeffrey's Silicon Valley experience includes roles as Vice President of Product Management, Vice President of Engineering, and Chief Evangelist. He has also worked as an independent consultant on topics including corporate strategy, product management, marketing, and interaction design. Jeffrey is based in London and is currently Managing Director of TIM Group, an Acuris Company. He also runs the London Organisational Learning Meetup and is a CTO mentor through CTO Craft.